Stephen Beaumont's
BREWPUB COOKBOOK

Stephen Beaumont's
BREWPUB COOKBOOK

100 GREAT RECIPES FROM 30 FAMOUS
NORTH AMERICAN BREWPUBS

Stephen Beaumont

AN IMPRINT OF BREWERS PUBLICATIONS
BOULDER, COLORADO

Siris Books
PO Box 1679, Boulder, CO 80306-1679
(303) 447-0816; Fax (303) 447-2825

Printed in the United States of America
10 9 8 7 6 5 4 3 2 1

ISBN 0-937381-64-0

Siris Books. Who is Siris? She was the daughter of Ninkasi, the Sumerian goddess of beer. Anthropologists personify Ninkasi as the filler of the cup, the one who pours the beer. Siris is the beer itself. Because she represents the presence and cultural importance of beer throughout civilization, this mysterious and little-known deity seemed perfect as the name of our new imprint.

Please direct all inquiries to the above address.

Library of Congress Cataloging-in-Publication Data
Beaumont, Stephen, 1964–
    [Brewpub cookbook]
    Stephen Beaumont's brewpub cookbook : 100 great recipes from 30 famous
    North American brewpubs.
        p.   cm.
    ISBN 0-937381-64-0 (alk. paper)
    1. Cookery. 2. Cookery (Beer). 3. Beer—United States. 4. Beer—Canada.
    5. Microbreweries—United States. 6. Microbreweries—Canada. I. Title.
    TX714.B386   1998
    641.5—dc21
                                                                    97-47323
                                                                    CIP

To my father and mother, Richard and Jean Beaumont.

BREWPUBS REPRESENTED IN THIS BOOK
30 BREWPUBS IN 2 COUNTRIES, 26 CITIES, 12 STATES:

- Boston Beer Works, Boston, MA
- Bushwakker Brewing Co., Regina, Saskatchewan
- C'est What Brewery, Toronto, Ontario
- Crescent City Brewhouse, New Orleans, LA
- Denison's Brewing Company & Restaurant, Toronto, Ontario
- Dock Street Brewing Co., Philadelphia, PA
- Globe Brewery & Barbecue Co., Globe, AZ
- Goose Island Brewing Company, Chicago, IL
- Gordon Biersch Brewing Co.:
  - Honolulu, HI
  - San Francisco, CA
  - Palo Alto, CA
  - Pasadena, CA
- Granite Brewery:
  - Halifax, Nova Scotia
  - Toronto, Ontario
- Great Lakes Brewing Co., Cleveland, OH
- Hale's Ales Brewery, Ltd., Seattle, WA
- The Kingston Brewing Company, Kingston, Ontario
- Marin Brewing Company, Larkspur, CA
- McMenamins Edgefield Estate, The Black Rabbit Restaurant, Troutdale, OR
- The Mendocino Brewing Company, Hopland, CA
- The Norwich Inn, Norwich, VT
- Pepperwood Bistro, Burlington, Ontario
- The Pike Pub and Brewery, Seattle, WA
- Portland Brewing Company, Brewhouse, Taproom and Grill, Portland, OR
- Pyramid Alehouse & Thomas Kemper Brewery, Seattle, WA
- The Redhook Ale Brewery and Forecaster Public House, Woodinville, WA
- The Rogue Ales Public House, Newport, OR
- Spinnakers Brew Pub, Victoria, BC
- Stoudt's Black Angus Restaurant, Adamstown, PA
- Swans Hotel and Pub/Buckerfield's Brewery, Victoria, BC
- The Twenty Tank Brewery, San Francisco, CA
- The Vermont Pub & Brewery, Burlington, VT
- Wynkoop Brewing Company, Denver, CO
- Zip City Brewing Company, New York, NY

CONTENTS

ACKNOWLEDGMENTS

First and foremost, I would like to thank the chefs at the contributing brewpubs for taking the time out of their busy schedules to answer my occasionally urgent requests for recipes. You all came through with flying colors, as I knew you would, and this book would be nowhere without your help.

I would also like to thank the people at Macmillan Canada, particularly my editor, Nicole de Montbrun. And gratitude is due to a great book designer, Kevin Connolly, who makes my words look so good on the page.

Finally, writing a cookbook is a lot more difficult than you might think and this particular cookbook would have been a whole lot harder were it not for one person, my wife Christine. From inputting recipes to kitchen testing assistance to putting up with me in the final weeks of my deadline, Christine provided help and support that was nothing short of invaluable. Thank you so very much, my love.

INTRODUCTION

WHY A BREWPUB
COOKBOOK?

In North America today, we have recently grown rather accustomed to the concept of the brewpub. In fact, save for certain small localities, the idea of a pub or restaurant that brews its own beer fresh for consumption on the premises has been enthusiastically embraced continent wide, with brewpubs opening up in locations as varied and diverse as Canmore, Alberta (pop. 6,000), and New York City (pop. 16.2 million). So great has been the commercial success of this concept that as I write these words in the fall of 1996, there are some 800 or more brewpubs scattered across Canada and the United States.

But by their very nature, brewpubs are about beer. Even the component parts of the name "brewpub" do not set the mouth to watering in anticipation of platefuls of luxurious food; the word "brew" being immediately connected with beer, which in turn is only rarely associated with food in North American culture, and "pub" being a term borrowed from the Brits that conjures up images of such hearty but basic fare as fish-and-chips, roast beef sandwiches and steak and kidney pie. So the question is repeated: why a cookbook that features recipes from this continent's brewpubs?

The answer to that query begins with beer. For beer truly is a food, and a profoundly good food at that. Beer is flavorful, to the point that some say it is blessed with a much wider range of sensory stimuli than is even wine. And beer is nutritious. Beer may be bitter or sweet, heavy or light, potent or benign, refreshing or fulfilling. In short, beer may be almost anything the brewer desires it to be, even spiced or fruit flavored! In this sense, the brewer, much more than the wine maker or distiller, is like the chef; constantly creating, altering, remaking and perfecting. Indeed, it is often said in brewing circles that if you can enjoy and understand the basics of cooking, then you are well on your way to becoming a fine brewer.

Is it any wonder then, that great brewpubs can usually be counted on to produce great food? It has certainly been my experience in my many dozens, if not hundreds of brewpub visits, that the finer the beer in a brewpub, the better the fare will be, as well. It only makes sense; if an establishment takes pride in the beer they put into the glass, it follows that they must also take great pride in the fare that they put on the plate. Because after all, both are food.

In my opinion, great food alone is not enough to make a great cookbook, and herein lies another reason for a brewpub cookbook. Just as the beers offered by this continent's many fine brewpubs range dramatically in their styles, so too does the food reflect the immense range of thought and inclination of the brewpub chefs and owners. The food, like the beer, is not only good, it is varied.

In my travels, I have enjoyed many different types of cuisine at many different types of brewpubs. I have enjoyed Chinese, Japanese and Thai foods; relished bratwurst, Creole chicken and *rillettes de porc*; and dined on pub grub, bistro cuisine and trattoria fare. And I have done all of this at brewpubs.

With this background, I knew right from the start that compiling a cookbook such as this would take more than a small amount of care. I immediately sensed, for example, that it would not be enough to merely include recipes solicited from random brewpubs. If this were to be a useful cookbook, I felt that it would be my duty and obligation to make sure that the brewpubs from which I gathered recipes represented the full diversity contained within the industry. For this reason, the brewpub selection process became perhaps the hardest part of creating this book.

There were disappointments of course — my original list of 38 brewpubs eventually dwindled down to the 30 represented in these pages — but for the most part, the brewpubs were highly cooperative and the diversity I aimed for was eventually achieved. But diversity was only a part of the equation as I saw it; there were other qualities I had to look for in brewpub selection.

I felt that each recipe in this book should stand not just as an endorsement of the food, but also of the brewpub, its beer and its place within the short history of the modern North American brewpub. As such, even as I was conscious of the need to reflect the industry's variety within my brewpub list, I knew also that I needed to represent the finest that the craft-brewing industry had to offer. These are the brewpubs represented in these pages.

I cannot say that these brewpubs on my list are the best in North America, because to make such a statement I would have had to visit every brewpub on the continent, all 800 plus of them, and I most definitely have not done that. What I will say, however, is that they all stand as among the best, recognized by patrons, writers and brewers alike as members of an elite class of brewpubs. Each one, for reasons as varied as their cuisines, has earned itself a place at the front of the book when the history of this craft-beer renaissance is one day finally written.

WHAT MAKES A BREWPUB SPECIAL?

The common ground upon which all of these brewpubs stand is that not one of them might be classified as an "ordinary" business, or at least, not in the way that one would classify car dealerships, real estate offices or hardware stores as such. They are each much more than the sum total of their wood, chrome and brass; they are reflections of the people who own them, work in them and eat, drink and socialize in them. And because the house-brewed beer personalizes the brewpub in a way unmatched by ordinary bars and restaurants, attending one of these brewpubs is very much akin to visiting someone's home.

The men and women who own and operate these "homes" are, without exception, innovators, dreamers and believers. They are individuals who understand and appreciate that great beer and fine food must always walk hand in hand and who know that in the same way that a beer is never "just a beer," neither should a brewpub ever be "just a brewpub." When you get to know brewpub owners and brewers as I have, you quickly realize that passion is very much a key ingredient in everything they do.

That passion is quite naturally reflected in their devotion to the beer that they brew, whether they do the brewing themselves, like Kevin Keefe of the Granite Brewery in Halifax, or just have an intense, personal commitment to it, like Paul Shipman of Seattle's Redhook Ale Brewery. It is also represented in the food that they allow to leave their brewpub kitchens. Even though few brewpub owners or operators have any direct role to play within the kitchens of their establishments, they are as committed to their brewpub's fare as any three-star French chef is to his or her cuisine.

This is the third and final reason for this book. For passion is not only a quality that deserves its own reward, it is also something that is usually very rewarding. And in addition to being deliciously flavorful and stylistically diverse, the recipes presented in the following pages are also uniformly the result of a very passionate commitment to great food and drink. Not coincidentally, they are also very rewarding. Try a few; I think that you will see what I mean.

ON COOKING
AND DINING
WITH BEER

Of all the beverages in the world, it is my contention that none other can equal beer's aptitude as a drink for any time and any occasion. Think of any time or any place or any celebration, and I will suggest a beer that is ideally suited in flavor, taste or attitude to complement the circumstances ideally. Be it a 50th birthday party or a lazy Sunday brunch, a music festival or a formal dinner, there exists a beer that will not only look, smell and taste right for the time, but will also feel right.

To further this belief, I have in the past written numerous stories about matching beer to everything from fine art to fine cuisine, and much of what lies in between. While some of these articles have been rather frivolous — even I don't bother worrying about whether the beer I'm drinking matches the music I'm playing or the video movie I'm watching — they do serve to illustrate the idea that beer is a supremely socially flexible and accommodating drink. Quite simply, beer can do it all.

It is in the kitchen and at the table, however, that beer reaches its zenith of perfection. To my mind, there does not exist a beverage more suited to cooking or dining than beer — not milk, not spirits, not even wine. The only unfortunate part of this equation is that beer's aptitude in these fields continues to pass unacknowledged in many, if not most, gastronomic circles. It is my hope that this cookbook will go at least a small way towards ameliorating that oversight.

BEER IN THE KITCHEN...

As a cooking liquid, beer is second only to water in its versatility. You may argue that milk has its strengths in that department, and it does, but would you use milk in a chili? Probably not. Wine certainly has its uses in the kitchen, but could you imagine blending wine with chocolate ice cream to make a dessert shake? The mere idea is enough to make a person cringe! And while cream has a role to play, its very nature, its creaminess, by definition disqualifies it from many diverse applications. No, for general cooking utility, it is very hard to compare anything with beer.

What gives beer its edge over other beverages in the ingredient department is exactly the opposite of what gives water its advantage. Where water is adept as a cooking liquid or component part of almost any dish because of its blandness and lack of definable character, beer's benefits as an ingredient stem from the remarkably wide and varied range of flavors and aromas available within its many, many styles and their even greater number of interpretations. Whatever the needs of the dish, chances are that beer has the flavors to fit the bill.

As illustrated by dozens of the recipes in this book, beer can play a role in any kind of dish, be it an appetizer, soup, salad, main course or dessert. For the above-mentioned chocolate shake, for example, a rich imperial stout or fruity Belgian ale would be marvelous. When making a vinaigrette for a green salad, skip or halve the vinegar and substitute a gueuze or acidic framboise instead. For a chowder, try using a sweetish brown ale along with the cream, or perk up a beef broth with a little dry stout. And whether you are steaming, braising, broiling, baking or frying, a little beer will go a long way to enliven any recipe. At the risk of invoking old clichés, beer not only is good food, it also makes food good.

This is not to say, however, that you will necessarily be able to taste the beer in every dish you use it in. In fact, the truth is quite the opposite; most beer cuisine recipes display little or no perceptible beer flavor in the finished product. Far from being a detriment, though, the reason for this apparent failing is precisely beer's greatest boon as an ingredient.

While one hates to use words like "magical" or "phenomenal" to characterize something that so many of us take quite for granted, the function of beer in cooking calls for exactly those kind of descriptives. For just as the brewing process was at one time viewed as alchemy of a sort, so does the role of beer in the kitchen relate to a kind of alchemic magic.

The way this magic works hinges upon the way that beer functions in relation to other ingredients in the cooking process. For reasons that are probably best explained by a chemist and which, to my mind, should not be explored for precisely that reason, beer acts almost perfectly as what I call a harmonizing ingredient in food. This is to say that beer will take any logical combination of ingredients and bond them together to form a taste that is much more than the sum total of its constituent parts. In effect, what beer does is to act as a medium for the other flavors, rather than trying to assert its own taste. Very unselfish, this beverage we call beer.

To illustrate how this harmonization occurs, simply make a basic stew using beef, carrots, onion, celery and herbs. Now, dividing the stew in half, add beef broth to one pot and equal parts of beef broth and stout to the other, and let the two stews simmer for an hour or so. Then, taste each stew and note how they differ. Even if you are not able to pinpoint the flavor of the stout exactly, which you may or may not be able to do depending on how much beer you used, rest assured that the differences between the dishes come strictly from the role beer played as a flavor medium in the second stew.

(If you are vegetarian, or just don't like beef stew, the same experiment can be easily carried out with a tomato sauce or vegetarian chili. Just cut back on the liquid used in one pot and add instead a brown ale or porter. The differences in the finished dishes should be just as apparent as they are in the stew example.)

While you might gather from the above explanation of beer's role in cooking that the style of beer used might be of only marginal importance, the reality is, in fact, quite the opposite. Selecting the right style of beer for the type of food being cooked is the most important choice a beer chef can make.

Within the world of beer, there exist literally dozens upon dozens of different generalized styles, from light lager to ebony stout and spiced dunkel weizen to fruit-flavored ale. And within each of these styles, there are numerous interpretations based on region, brewing method and consumer tastes, to say nothing of the personal preferences of the brewer. Given all of this plenty from which to choose, it seems obvious that it would be the height of folly to list as a recipe ingredient something described quite simply as "beer," but this is exactly what occurs in all too many recipes.

To be fair, many of the recipes that generically itemize "beer" among their ingredients are holdovers from a time in North America, not all that long ago, when we did not recognize the plentiful array of beer styles because we had no access to them. Today, however, in the midst of the craft-beer renaissance and its cornucopia of available beer styles, there is no excuse for calling for "beer" in a recipe. What style should we use — roasty stout or spritzy wheat beer, intensely flavorful doppelbock or refreshing pilsner? With all of the dramatically different beers we now have at hand, this is no idle query.

So we need a stylistic guideline for cooking with beer, and fortunately, a simple one does exist. As a general rule, it says, it is always a good idea to use a beer style that emulates the basic character of the dish. Hence, when looking for a beer to use in a heavy and hearty stew recipe, a robust ale such as an oatmeal stout or rich brown ale makes for a wise addition. Conversely, when seeking a beer to go into a fruit flan, a fruit-flavored wheat beer or particularly fruity Belgian dubbel ale will fulfil the need most admirably. And so it goes; acidic gueuze in a vinaigrette, light weizen for white fish, brown ale for gravies, and so on.

As with any guideline, of course, familiarity will breed contempt and more experienced beer chefs often delight in employing beers that would not necessarily be intuitively connected to certain foods. In this fashion, we end up with salmon poached in apricot ale, cabbage cooked in pale ale and spicy chimichangas made with pilsner. However, such dishes should be considered the exceptions that prove the rule.

Because beer works so well as a medium and flavor enhancer, rather than as a prominent taste ingredient, beer-based cuisine can even be enjoyed by non-beer drinkers. During the time that I was kitchen testing all of the recipes for this book, my wife and I hosted her sister and father for a weekend and decided to try out a number of cookbook-destined dishes while they were here. The only catch to our plan was that Armand Haley, my father-in-law, is an abstainer and has been since he was just a kid. This was truly to be the test of my theory.

With only two exceptions, all of the recipes we cooked that weekend passed muster with flying colors. Of the exceptions, one was a bread recipe made with a pale ale that contributed a slight bitterness to the finished loaf, which Armand said he did not especially enjoy but neither could he identify as a beer flavor, and the other a porter cheesecake that got a thumbs down only because he does not particularly like cream cheese. Both dishes, I should add, got enthusiastic endorsements from the rest of the table and the cheesecake was such a hit with Christine's sister, Corrine, that we sent her home with a large slice, which she threatened to eat in one sitting. It was just that good.

But while taste is one thing, what might well be of greater concern to the abstainer is the alcohol in beer and the possibility that it might transfer to the completed dish. While this is an understandable apprehension, it is a completely groundless one in most cases where beer is used in cooking. This is because as long as there is a cooking process involved in the creation of a dish, the heat used will quickly evaporate the alcohol, leaving in play only the flavors, aromas and harmonizing qualities of the beer. Exceptions to this rule are to be found in salad dressings, certain dips and spreads, no-bake desserts and other recipes in which there is no oven, broiler, stove or other heat source used in the preparation process. However, in many of these instances, a quick turn on the stove will efficiently rid your dish of alcohol while altering the basic character of the recipe only minimally.

Two other points about cooking with beer that deserve mention concern the quantity and quality of the beer used. All too often, I have spoken with, or heard of, people who will cook with only bottle-sized quantities of beer or will use only beer that they would not bother to drink themselves, justifying its use on the premise that "it's no good for drinking, so I might as well cook with it." These are, in fact, the two biggest woes afflicting the would-be beer chef.

On the quantity front, although it is self-evident, it bears mentioning that beer is a liquid. As such, disproportionately large quantities of it will thin the character of whatever is being made and dilute the taste. This need not be the case. In many instances, only a very slight amount of beer is necessary and in others, the intense flavors of the beer employed will be such that less beer is required than would be immediately apparent. In every conceivable instance, then, it is far better to proceed with a light and easy hand rather than with a heavy one, recognizing that it is much simpler to add beer than it is to try to remove it. And as chef and author Candy Schermerhorn once observed during one of our many long-distance conversations, whether a dish calls for a pint or a teaspoon of beer, the amount used does not in any way detract from the ability of the dish to qualify as beer cuisine.

Equally important as the quantity of the beer used in a dish is its quality. For even though the full flavor of a beer, or lack thereof, might not be apparent in what eventually makes it to the bowl or the plate, its merits or defects will still be evident for all to taste. To understand this, you need only direct your thoughts for a moment to the humble tomato.

During the fall tomato harvest, when plump and juicy beefsteaks can be plucked straight from the vine still warm from the sun's ripening rays, tomato-based dishes positively explode with luxurious taste and aroma, and even a dish in which the tomato plays only a supporting role is made that much better by the fresh, flavorful fruit. Now, contrast dishes made from fall's tomato bounty with ones made with winter tomatoes, sold at the market in a greenish yellow, pre-ripened state and stuck in a brown paper bag or placed on a windowsill until a reluctant red creeps into their skins. This time, those dishes that previously daz-zled, now merely fuel, with the flat tomato character evident even where minimal quantities are used. So it is with the tomato, and so it is with beer.

Plainly stated, if you use a lesser beer in your cooking, a lesser dish will result. There are no exceptions to this rule and it is only when you are willing to settle for a somewhat second-rate end product that you should cook with inferior beer. Chefs who cook with wine have an axiom they use for selecting their ingre-dients and it applies equally to the use of beer in the kitchen: never cook with a beer you would not yourself drink.

...AND AT THE TABLE

If beer's ability to partner with food ended in the kitchen, that alone would be enough to qualify it as a spectacular and worthy addition to any gourmet's refrig-erator and cellar. But the tremendous versatility of this great beverage does not stop there; as a mealtime companion, beer is every bit as versatile, every bit as harmonious and every bit as delicious.

As a society, North Americans tend to give short shrift to the notion of beer as a mealtime accompaniment. From our earliest days at the dining room table, we are taught to believe that when a special meal is put on the table, the beer is put away and wine is brought out. It is a response that in most of us, is so ingrained, it may even be considered conditioned.

To understand our food and wine fixation, you need look no further than France. Because, for many of us, our first truly formal dining experience, and that of our mothers and fathers, came at a French restaurant, with French cuisine on the plate and, yes, French wine in the glass. So, too, was it for so many of us when we were first learning how to cook, with French cuisine cookbooks at our sides and the expectation—no, obligation!—that we would serve wine to our guests when the meal was brought to the table. It was a simple progression of assump-tions: the French were responsible for the best food we knew; the French drank wine with their meals; and so therefore we should also drink wine with our meals.

Now, stop and think for a moment what might have happened had we received our gastronomic tutelage from a brewing country such as Germany instead of a wine-producing one like France. Perhaps, just perhaps, we would be sitting down for our important meals with steins of lager or märzen instead of glasses of Bordeaux or Côtes du Rhône.

It is a facile example, I will admit, and one that ignores the fact that the French almost single-handedly brought the art of cuisine to the whole of the Western world, not just North America in this century. But it does, I believe, serve to illustrate my point that the consumption of wine at the table is more of a social imperative than a gastronomic one. Were it otherwise, we would most certainly drink beer with our meals.

Many devotees of the grape would no doubt take issue with the notion that beer is more adept and more versatile at partnering with foods than is wine, but it is true. Not that it is any fault of wine, mind you, just that beer, by its very nature, offers more flexibility of tastes, aromas and textures than may be found in fermented grape juice. As noted in the cooking section above, beer can be brewed in an almost infinite number of ways and may even incorporate fruits, spices and herbs of all sorts, whereas wine can only be made of grapes. Even taking into account the variable skill levels that may be put on display by the brewer or wine maker — which is not to say that one discipline is more difficult than the other, just that there exist a wide range of differently skilled individuals in both fields — it would seem obvious that beer has more flexibility when it comes to complementing the flavors of food.

For the skeptics still among us, I have a simple question: what wine matches well with chocolate? If you answered port, you have read the superb book, *Red Wine With Fish* by David Rosengarten and Joshua Wesson, but I'm not sure that you have correctly answered the question. This is because Wesson and Rosengarten go to great pains to explain that their chocolate-port matches require a dessert of low to moderate sweetness with something acidic, such as fruit, included in the dish to help out the wine. With beer, no such qualifiers are necessary. When you partner pure Belgian chocolate with a full-bodied abbey-style ale or match a rich chocolate cake with a robust imperial stout, you have magic, pure and simple.

Neither are there qualifiers necessary when other traditionally non-wine friendly foods require a complementary beer partner. Salad with vinaigrette? Match the acidity of the dressing with a gueuze or framboise. Artichoke? The chemical in the artichoke that makes subsequent flavors taste sweeter plays havoc with wine, but has a negligible impact on a well-structured best bitter or soft, British-style pale ale. Omelets and other egg dishes? A Belgian- or German-style wheat beer is perfect, with the one you choose determined purely by how fatty the dish is — Belgian white beer for lower-fat scrambled eggs and German weizen for higher-fat cheese omelets.

There is one area, however, where beer falls flat on its face as a mealtime partner, and that is in the field of common knowledge. The rules that supposedly govern dining with wine are well known: red wine with meat and white wine with fish, Stilton with port, champagne and caviar, never serve wine with artichoke and so on. Indeed, these tenets are so well known that authors like Rosengarten and Wesson have written entire books debunking some of the mythology that has been built up around the practice. The same, unfortunately, can hardly be said about beer.

North American society has spent so much time building up the image of beer as a fun-time, common-people drink that we have come very close to completely losing any vision of beer that might be considered contradictory. As such, when the subject of dining with beer is raised, even many industry insiders and proponents of the idea become confounded and confused. In the absence of a basic set of guidelines, the average beer aficionado doesn't stand a chance.

It was for this reason that I introduced four basic beer and food pairing maxims in my book, *A Taste for Beer*, and I think that they bear repeating here. They are based upon tried and true gastronomic verities and although they by no means stand hard and fast and unalterable, they do provide a good base from which to begin.

1. THINK "RED WINE" FOR ALE AND "WHITE WINE" FOR LAGER

Because so many people are familiar with the somewhat flawed but nonetheless useful dictate of "red wine, with meat, white wine with fish and poultry," a convenient way to begin matching beer with your food is to think of ale as you would red wine, and lager as white. Although like the wine rule, it is fraught with loopholes, as a general guide, it does provide a safe place to start.

In many instances, ale behaves with food in much the same way as would red wine. Thus, if you had a rare to medium roast beef and were thinking about serving a good Côtes du Rhône with it, you would get equally favorable results by substituting a full-bodied brown ale or a malty Scottish ale. Similarly, a hamburger tastes that much better when accompanied by a pint of best bitter, lamb is raised to new gastronomic heights by a glass of strong, malty ale and a piece of good Stilton tastes heavenly beside a snifter of barley wine.

On the flip side, lager will most often fill the role of a white wine most ably, frequently producing results superior to those of the wine. With a delicate piece of pan-fried whitefish, for example, a lightish German-style pilsner would provide a stunning accompaniment. So it also goes with chicken, where a Bohemian pilsner can deliciously fill the role of a Chablis, and the seemingly endless controversy over whether to serve white or red wine with roast pork can be resolved by offering instead a good märzen.

There are, however, rather severe limits to this relationship. To begin with, where the red and white descriptives do cover most wines, taken in their narrow stylistic definition, lager and ale leave out entire classes of beer such as wheats, stouts and bocks. Also, as with the wine rule, such a myopic view of food and beverage pairings excludes a good many wonderful relationships which, while on the surface may look odd or even bizarre, are actually quite satisfying and delicious. Just one such example from the beer world is the exquisite way in which stout and smoked salmon complement one another, making a heavenly match that would never be permitted within the boundaries of the above rule.

2. TREAT BITTERNESS IN BEER AS YOU WOULD ACIDITY IN WINE

This simple rule, again dependant on an understanding of the basic wine maxims, makes matching beer to any spicy, salty or oily foods a simple affair. Just remember that the bitterness in beer should increase proportionally to the level of spice, salt or oil in the food and you should be fine.

To illustrate how this relationship works, you will need a hoppy beer such as a pale ale, a malty Scottish ale or similar style and a bag of salted pretzels. Try eating the pretzels with the malty beer first, and then with the hoppy ale. What you will find is that the bitterness of the pale ale will offset the saltiness of the pretzels and allow all of the flavors to blend harmoniously. The malty beer, on the other hand, will be possessed of a sweetness that will be in conflict with the salt on the pretzel, thus causing beer and pretzel alike to taste flat and unappetizing.

The one place where the bitterness-acidity parallel falls apart is when acidic fruit like tomatoes, oranges or limes are brought into the picture. This is due to the fact that although bitterness can act like acidity, it is not acidic itself and therefore will not provide a complementary component to balance the natural acidity in such foods. In most other food and beer matching situations, however, the analogy will hold.

3. COMPLEMENT OR CONTRAST

This maxim is a food pairing basic that applies whether you wish to partner beer with steak, wine with seafood or a sauce with a casserole. When searching for flavors in beer that will most appropriately accompany the flavors of a dish, try to find those that will provide either a contrasting relationship or a complementary one.

On the complementary side of this equation, the idea is to find taste sensations that will enhance and embellish each other and so raise the overall flavor and enjoyment of the meal. One example of this may be found in the way that a robust and malty ale will echo the full and flavorful character of a hearty beef stew, which is not to say that the ale would taste beefy, but that it would have a richness similar to that of the stew. When these two flavors meet on the palate, the big body of the ale will play up the character of the gravy in the stew and the beef's sweetish, meaty taste will further enrich the body of the beer. It works because each sip of beer or taste of stew augments the qualities of the other, building their combined characters up to a pinnacle of flavor.

Where contrast is concerned, the desired effect is quite the opposite. Usually used where the flavors of the food are particularly sharp or intense, a beer's contrasting taste serves to provide a respite from the strength of the food and also to refresh the palate between bites. One example of how this relationship works is found in the marvelous way in which a hoppy pilsner will provide contrast to the rich, sweet creaminess of a chowder or heavy cream soup. With the dryness of the beer serving to cleanse and refresh the palate between spoonfuls of soup, the odds that the luxurious creaminess of the soup might become overwhelming are severely minimized.

4. ALWAYS HAVE AN EQUAL OR GREATER LEVEL OF SWEETNESS IN THE BEER

Designed for desserts, this maxim works equally well when particularly sweet soups or casseroles are presented at the table. The point of this one is to avoid having the taste perception of the beer turn comparatively bitter or sour because the food with which you are drinking it is overly sweet. It is a simple case of an unwanted contrast.

When two sweet tastes are presented together, the sweeter one will normally have the effect of making the other appear to be less sweet than it is in reality. Where beer and food matches are concerned, the sweeter beer will have the positive effect of toning down the overall sweetness of the dessert and thereby allowing some of the other flavors in the dish — be they chocolate, fruit or whatever — to come fully to the palate. In the reverse scenario, however, the effect is not so positive. Because virtually all beers brewed today have some level of hopping, the sweeter dessert will moderate the maltiness of the beer and allow the bitter hop component to come into play. And because bitter and sweet are not necessarily cooperative taste sensations, that bitterness can quickly turn into at best, a flavor-flattening earthiness or, at worst, a high level of perceived sourness.

Exceptions do exist to this sweetness tenet — chocolate, for example, will pair well with some stouts even if the sweetness component is greater in the chocolate — but for the most part, it is a wise guideline to follow. Admittedly, it is unlikely to save you time as you race around your city or town trying to find beers high in sweetness, but it will prevent those that you do locate from tasting like lesser beers than they really are.

BEER AND FOOD PAIRINGS*

Although each recipe in this book has a listed beermate — that is, a beer that will deliciously complement the dish — you may have other ideas in mind when it comes to beer and food pairing. The following chart, then, is a handy listing of basic foodstuffs and the beers that best complement them.

*For a more detailed look at matching beer with food, please see my previous book, A Taste for Beer (Macmillan Canada, 1995).

SOUPS

Cream soup   *Hoppy pilsners*
Mulligatawny soup   *British-style pale ale*
French onion soup   *Scotch ale*
Beef vegetable soup   *English brown ale or porter*
Minestrone   *Vienna lager*
Lobster bisque   *Kölsch*

SALADS

Green salad w/ vinaigrette   *Hoppy brown ale*
Green salad w/ cream dressing   *Pilsner*
Fruit salad   *German-style hefeweizen*

RED MEAT

Roast beef   *British-style pale ale*
Roast beef with gravy   *Scottish ale*
Carbonade of beef   *Flemish brown ale*
Hearty beef stew   *Robust brown ale or Scottish ale*
Steak and kidney pie   *British-style pale ale*
Hamburger   *Amber ale*
Beef teriyaki   *Cream ale*
Roast leg of lamb   *Scottish ale*
Buffalo   *Porter*
Venison   *Mild brown ale*

POULTRY AND PORK

Roast chicken   *Dunkel lager*
Chicken Kiev   *Bohemian pilsner*
Chicken Cordon Bleu   *Märzen*
Roast duck   *Best bitter*
Roast pork   *Märzen*
Pork ribs w/ barbecue sauce   *Vienna lager*

SEAFOOD

Grilled or broiled whitefish   *Bohemian or German pilsner*
Barbecued salmon   *Dunkel lager or dry bock*
Smoked salmon   *Dry stout*
Raw oysters   *Stout*
Steamed mussels and clams   *The same beer as used for steaming*
Lobster or crab   *Stout or Bohemian pilsner*
Cajun-style shellfish   *Best bitter*
(boiled in heavily spiced water)

VEGETABLES

Corn-on-the-cob   *Canadian ale*
Broccoli   *German or Bohemian pilsner*
Cooked onion   *Vienna lager or amber ale*
Raw onion   *American pale ale or IPA*
Quiche Lorraine   *Wheat ale*
Falafel   *Alt*
Bruschetta   *Vienna lager*
Tomato   *Vienna lager*

EGG DISHES

Scrambled eggs   *Belgian-style wheat beer*
Eggs Benedict   *Weizen*
Cheese omelets   *Weizen or best bitter*
Farmer's breakfast   *Oatmeal stout*

DESSERT

Chocolate pudding or mousse *Oatmeal stout*
Flourless chocolate cake *Imperial stout*
Chocolate pudding cake *Sweet stout or barley wine*
Plain Belgian chocolate *Belgian abbey ale*
Chocolate cheesecake *Scotch ale*
Cherry pie *Kriek*
Raspberry crumble *Raspberry wheat beer*
Bananas Foster *Weizen*
Trifle *Strong fruit ale*
Lemon meringue pie *American wheat ale or weizen*
Christmas pudding *Strong, spiced ale*

CHEESE

Cream cheese with pepper *German pilsner*
Edam *Wheat ale*
French Brie *Dry Stout*
Stilton *Barley wine or old ale*
Canadian cheddar *Best bitter*
Limburger *Doppelbock*
Danish blue cheese *Dry stout*
Smoked Gruyère *Rauchbier*

A GLOSSARY
OF BEER STYLES

Owing to the large number of beer styles mentioned in this cookbook and conscious of the fact that not everyone will be familiar with every style, I have assembled the following handy, quick-reference guide to beer styles and their flavors. Due to space restrictions, however, I have stopped well shy of providing an inclusive guide to the world of beer, as that could easily take up the pages of this and another book. Instead, I have focused on only those styles that are noted in the following recipes and dealt with them in only the most general terms of flavor and aroma.

While this abbreviated guide should be enough to steer you onto the right road when you are preparing any of these marvelous dishes, it does fall quite short of offering a definitive word on what makes one beer style different from the other. If you do wish to learn more about beer styles, there are numerous books on the market that go into the subject in much greater detail, including my own *A Taste For Beer*, Michael Jackson's *Beer Companion* and the new *Encyclopedia of World Beer* by Benjamin Myers and Graham Lees.

TOP-FERMENTED BEERS (ALE CLASS)

Alt Copper-brown in color with a moderately hoppy and earthy aroma. Moderately hopped and medium- to light-bodied with a dry character and an earthy bitterness and faint fruitiness.

American Amber Ale Medium gold to deep rust in color and widely varied in aroma and taste. The flavor should generally be more greatly influenced by malt than by hops and the character should be that of a "session beer," or an easy-drinking ale.

American Pale Ale Deep gold to amber brown in color with an assertively hoppy aroma showing floral, vegetal or occasionally citrus (grapefruit) notes. Forcefully bitter in taste but the strong hop character should be in balance with a good malty backbone.

Barley Wine Dark brown to mahogany in color with complex aromas of mulled fruit, nuts or even tanned leather. Moderate to forcefully bitter hop notes should be apparent in the body of this strong (7–11% alcohol by volume) ale, but these may be somewhat subdued by a strong sweetness holding some fruitiness and other malt notes.

Belgian-Style Abbey Ale (including site-specific Trappist ales) Earthy brown to mahogany in color with a rich and robust, often fruity, aroma. A broad class encompassing hoppy medium-strength ales (Orval) and robust, alcoholic ales (Chimay) alike. In general, look for a rich and full-bodied strong ale with complex, malt-dominated taste.

Belgian-Style Golden Ale Medium gold in color with an off-dry, spicy and sometimes lightly fruity aroma. The alcoholic strength (7–8% alcohol by volume) should be tempered by a dry, pear-like fruitiness, light spice and a somewhat refreshing character.

Belgian-Style Tripel Medium gold colored with a somewhat sweet to medium-dry and often lightly fruity aroma. Very strong (8–9% alcohol by volume) and para-doxically refreshing, they will tend to be lightly to moderately fruity in the body and clean and complex in character.

Best Bitter Amber to rust colored and moderately hoppy in aroma. The flavor should be evidently hoppy but in balance with a dryish malty character. A bitter should be softer and less assertive than a pale ale and traditionally lower in alcohol (3.5–4.5% alcohol by volume).

British Mild Ale Brown in color with a light and malty aroma, sometimes with lightly chocolaty notes. Low strength (3–3.5% alcohol by volume) with a mild, malty body occasionally holding lightly hoppy notes. Designed for easy, refreshing drinking.

British Pale Ale Medium brown in color with a floral, fruity or woody aroma. The taste is highlighted by high hopping rate but the resulting bitterness should be only moderate and in balance with fruity malt.

Brown Ale Medium to dark brown in color with a balanced, nutty-fruity and occasionally somewhat woody aroma. The flavor should be predominantly malty, but a certain degree of dryness is essential to the style, particularly in American interpretations of it.

Canadian Ale Medium gold in color with a balanced malt and hop aroma containing notes of fruit, subtle spice and grain. It should have a full and possibly slightly creamy character with a light fruitiness and, variably, a moderate degree of complex hoppiness or notes of spice.

Cream Ale Light to medium gold in color with a relatively well-hopped aroma showing some fruitiness. Its character should be fairly light and refreshing, similar to a lager, but with some ale-like fruitiness or round, malty character and a light to moderate hoppiness.

Dry Stout (also known as Irish Stout) Deep brown to jet black in color with a very roasty, sometimes coffee-ish dry aroma. It should be medium-bodied with a decidedly roasty flavor variously carrying licorice or coffee notes.

Extra Special Bitter (also known as ESB) Similar to the Best Bitter except with a little more of everything: malt, hops and alcohol.

Flavored Ale In North America, ales have been flavored with everything from nuts to honey and watermelon to maple syrup. Sometimes the flavor of these adjuncts will be little in evidence, as with many honey beers, and in other instances they will be dominant, as with some maple beers. See also Fruit Wheat.

Imperial Stout (also known as Russian Stout) Jet black in color and rich and complex in aroma, holding a complicated mix of malt and hop notes. Rich and potent (8–12% alcohol by volume) in the body with a forceful, complex, alcoholic and even winey flavor.

India Pale Ale (also known as IPA) The strongest (5.5% alcohol or more by volume) member of the pale ale class with a forceful hop presence showing in both the aroma and taste. Light gold to pale amber in color and quite bitter in flavor.

Irish Ale Medium brown in color with perhaps a reddish tinge and aromatically soft and lightly caramely or chocolaty, with perhaps a hint of fruitiness. The flavor should be roundly malty with fruitiness and a somewhat buttery character.

Kölsch Light to medium gold in color with a fresh and lightly fruity aroma. A finesse beer with a delicate maltiness and a light, acidic hopping drying it out to a refreshing, faintly herbal character.

Oatmeal Stout Black in color with a lightly sweet, often porridgey aroma holding notes of roast and occasionally caramelized sugar. The body is rich and full, with a character that is best described as silky. The flavor will be sweetish and hold roasty and possibly coffee notes.

Old Ale (also known as Strong Ale) Rust to dark brown with potent aromas containing a variety of fruits, varying degrees of hoppiness and occasionally winey or whisky-ish alcoholic notes. Of moderate to high strength (6.5% alcohol and up by volume) with a complex character of fruit, nuts and many other flavors in a full body.

Porter Dark brown in color with varying degrees of roastiness and a fair dose of coffee, chocolate, anise or soft fruitiness, or a combination of the four, in the aroma. The taste should be roasty and chocolaty and the body should be mildly to moderately full.

Saison Medium gold in color and effervescent with a fresh, citrus and occasionally somewhat leafy aroma. Designed for summer drinking, the saison will be dry, sometimes tart or barnyardy in character and very refreshing.

Scotch Ale Dark brown to purplish black in color with a very sweet and malty, sometimes almost treacly aroma. Strong (7–8% alcohol by volume), full-bodied and warming with a malty complexity defining the taste.

Scottish Ale Amber to medium brown in color with a caramely or toffeeish malty aroma. Decidedly sweetish in taste, there should be minimal hop bitterness and occasionally a mild roastiness.

Smoked Ale A variation on the traditional Bamberg Rauchbier (see separate entry) in which ales of varying styles are brewed using smoked barley malt. Lightly to heavily smoky in aroma and flavor.

Spiced Ale A very broad category encompassing everything from traditional Belgian ales seasoned with coriander, allspice, ginger and other spices to New World spiced ales including the popular pumpkin-pie-spiced beers.

Strong Porter Dark brown to black in color with a sweetish, roasty and often somewhat sugary aroma. Strong in alcohol content (7–8% alcohol by volume) but lightish in body, often showing cherry, plum or port-like notes.

BOTTOM-FERMENTED BEERS (LAGER CLASS)

Bock Amber rust in color with a sweetish, sometimes chocolaty aroma holding no bitter hop notes. The flavor of this strong (6–7.5% alcohol by volume) style should be sweet without being fruity, with notes of chocolate, mocha and/or spice.

Bohemian Pilsner Light gold in color with a floral, hoppy aroma. The taste should be assertively dry but also soft and floral with a balancing malt backbone and a lingering hop finish.

Doppelbock A stronger (7.5% alcohol by volume and up) style of bock with a deeper, richer color and a sweeter and more characterful aroma. The flavor will be sweet and intense, with occasional berry or winey notes amid great complexity.

Dortmunder Export (also known as Export) Light to medium gold in color with the hopping asserting itself slightly more than the malt in the aroma. The flavor is a balanced combination of crisp hopping and fairly forceful malt, resulting in a moderately full body of just above-average strength (5–5.5% alcohol by volume).

Dunkel (also known as Munich Dunkel or Münchner Dunkel) Medium to dark brown in color with a malt-dominated aroma holding a balancing, floral hoppiness. The flavor will also be malt dominated, with an off-dry and perhaps slightly spicy character holding mild to moderate chocolaty, roasty notes.

German Pilsner (also known as German Pils) Light gold in color and strongly hoppy in aroma, often with assertive woody or leafy notes. The body will be dry and refreshing, with a strong hop bitterness and a very light malt presence.

Maibock (also known as Pale Bock or Helles Bock) Medium gold to amber in color and sweet and sometimes lightly floral in aroma. The character should be fresh and at least somewhat refreshing, with light fruitiness but no notes of chocolate or mocha.

Munich Helles (also known as Münchner Hell) Light to medium gold in color with a fresh, malt-accented aroma with light notes of floral or perfumey hopping. The flavor is also malt-dominated, with a soft and rounded character and moderate strength (4.5–5% alcohol by volume).

Oktoberfest Märzen (also known as Festbier or Oktoberfestbier) Medium gold to medium brown in color with a malty, slightly spicy and sometimes modestly roasty aroma. The character should be generally similar to that of a Vienna Lager but with greater alcohol (5.5–6% alcohol by volume) and perhaps a light fruitiness and/or roastiness.

Rauchbier A traditional style of Bamberg brewed using barley malt that has been smoked over wood. Normally brewed in the Oktoberfest Märzen or Bock style, these beers range from moderate to very smoky in aroma and flavor.

Vienna Lager Amber red in color with a malty aroma showing toasty or spicy notes and possibly a light hopping. The character should be smooth and graceful with a sweet and spicy flavor and a subtle, drying hop present towards the finish.

Whisky Malt Beer (also known as Peated Malt Beer) Developed as a style in France, reportedly in response to the great popularity of Scottish malt whiskies. Medium to dark brown in color and light- to medium-bodied, with a sweet, malty and very lightly smoky, or more precisely, peaty aroma and flavor.

WHEAT BEERS (TOP-FERMENTED)

American Wheat Ale Light to medium gold in color with a light and grainy aroma holding varying degrees of citrus or spice notes. The body will be light and the flavor slightly sweet with notes of grain and lemon or spice appearing in varying degrees. These beers are sometimes labeled as Hefeweizens.

Dunkel Weizen Similar to a Hefeweizen except with a medium brown color and more of a complex spiciness in the aroma and flavor.

Fruit Lambic Spontaneously fermented Belgian lambics (young and aged versions of which are blended to make Gueuze; see separate entry) that have been flavored with fruit. Traditional styles are cherry-flavored Kriek and raspberry-flavored Framboise, but peach, black currant and other fruits are sometimes used.

Fruit Wheat New World wheat beers that are flavored with various different fruits. American Wheat Ales are most often used as the light flavor of the wheat allows the fruit to come through. See also Flavored Ale.

Gueuze Bright gold and often hazy, with a tart and citrus aroma, occasionally very sour and barnyardy. The flavor will be quite sour unless the beer has been sweetened with sugar, with complex tastes lurking below the tartness.

Hefeweizen (also known as Weizen or Weissebier; if filtered, Kristall Weizen) Light to medium gold in color with a full and spicy aroma carrying clove and/or banana notes. Refreshingly light and effervescent body with varying mixtures of clove, banana and citrus notes.

Weizenbock Medium to dark brown in color with assertive aromas filled with a complicated blend of fruity esters, especially banana, and spice, particularly clove. Strong (7–8% alcohol by volume), bananay or bubblegummy and very spicy in flavor.

White Beer (also known as Blanche, Belgian-style Wheat Beer or Wit) Shimmering sandy to pale gold in color with an orangey and spicy aroma, holding coriander notes in dominance. The character is very refreshing with a light combination of citrus fruit and coriander flavors, occasionally including other spice notes.

APPETIZERS & SIDE DISHES

Spiced Olives

From: C'est What Brewery, Winery and Restaurant
Toronto, Ontario, Canada

Created by Chef Jeff Sararas

Served alone, or as part of an antipasto plate, these olives are an absolute delight — the best I've tasted yet!

Beermate: With all of the intense flavors present in these delightful olives, picking a match is quite a challenge. I suggest the parallel intensity of a smoked beer like the Kaiserdom Rauchbier or Zip City Rauchbier.

Before You Begin: This marinade can make good olives great but it cannot make poor olives good, so start with olives of the highest quality for excellent results. And when the olives are all gone, the marinade can be used as a dressing for a great Greek salad.

> 2 cups vegetable oil
> 1 cup red wine vinegar
> 1/4 cup chopped fresh parsley
> 4 tbsp dried oregano
> 2 tbsp whole capers (optional)
> 1 tbsp chili flakes
> 1/2 tbsp Dijon mustard
> 4 cloves garlic, minced
> Salt and pepper to taste
> 5 cups kalamata olives, whole

In a large bowl, combine all of the ingredients except for the olives and whisk vigorously until well blended. Drain the olives well and place in any airtight container large enough to hold the total volume (about 10 cups) or divide them among several smaller containers. Pour the marinade over the olives to just cover, seal and refrigerate. Chill for 2 to 3 days, shaking the container(s) daily to remix and distribute the marinade before serving.

Makes about 10 cups.

Bruschetta

From: The Wynkoop Brewing Company
Denver, Colorado, USA

*Created by Executive Chef Big John Dickenson and
Chef de Cuisine David Allen*

The Cal-Ital food fad has made bruschetta into a very popular appetizer, but rarely is it done as decoratively and flavorfully as it is in this recipe.

Beermate: With the combined sweetness of the roasted garlic, sun-dried tomatoes and olive oil, this dish cries out for a contrasting influence. Give it one with a dry pilsner like Pilsner Urquell or the slightly sweeter Creemore Springs Lager.

Before You Begin: This is already an untraditional take on bruschetta, so feel free to make your own adjustments. Chefs Dickenson and Allen suggest that brie works well in place of the mozzarella and that roasted red peppers can ably substitute for the sun-dried tomatoes.

1 bulb garlic, trimmed at the root end
1 tbsp dry chardonnay
1 tbsp extra virgin olive oil
1 cup shredded mozzarella
1 tbsp coarsely chopped fresh basil
1 tbsp extra virgin olive oil
Salt and pepper to taste
1 cup sun-dried tomatoes
1 baguette
3/4 cup butter
1 tbsp dried oregano
1 tbsp dried thyme

Place the garlic bulb in a small metal pie tin, root side up, and drizzle with wine and olive oil. Bake at 350°F for 1 hour.

In a bowl, mix the mozzarella with the basil, olive oil, salt and pepper and refrigerate until ready to use.

If using dry sun-dried tomatoes, reconstitute them in a saucepan in 1 cup of hot water for 30 minutes before chopping. If using sun-dried tomatoes in oil, remove from the oil and julienne.

Slice the baguette in half lengthwise and slice on an angle to form points. Toast as much baguette as will be needed and reserve the rest for later. Melt the butter in a small pot and add the oregano and thyme. Brush the toasted points with the herb butter.

Separate the cloves of the baked garlic and squeeze the roasted paste into a small dish. Arrange the toast points on a platter surrounded by the marinated mozzarella, roasted garlic and julienned sun-dried tomatoes. Garnish with olives and pickled pepperoncini if desired and serve, encouraging everyone to make their own bruschetta.

Serves 4.

THE WYNKOOP BREWING COMPANY
1634 Eighteenth Street
Denver, Colorado, USA 80202
Phone: 303-297-2700

Among the denizens of the American craft-brewing industry, the Wynkoop Brewing Company of Denver may very well be the best-known brewpub on the continent. Oddly enough, though, this exalted status among brewers and brewery owners has little to do with the great ales and marvelous meals one can always expect at this large downtown brewpub. No, despite Wynkoop's considerable gastronomic achievements, it takes more than just great food and drink to make this kind of impression on the brewing community.

What it takes, apparently, is the seemingly boundless hospitality of the ever-cordial owner of Wynkoop, John Hickenlooper.

Each and every year, as the city of Denver plays host to the Great American Beer Festival — a monstrous beer event that in 1996 included more than 350 breweries and over 1450 beers — John Hickenlooper plays host to the industry side of the beer show equation. Oh sure, there may be an official hotel of the GABF and certain functions may have the signature stamp of the organization that runs the fest, but the Wynkoop is where the real headquarters resides. Be it eleven o'clock in the morning, six at night or two the following morning, a quick stroll through the brewpub or its upstairs pool hall is certain to bring you to the heart of the American craft-brewing industry. And nine times out of ten, John Hickenlooper will be there, shaking hands, greeting new friends and generally making everyone feel at home.

I met John during the run of my first GABF back in 1991, as he and Wynkoop's late and sadly missed brewer and co-owner, Russell Schehrer, welcomed brewers, brewery owners, beer press and beer aficionados alike into their pub. Despite the festival being held that year on the edge of town and there being several other brewpubs from which to choose in Denver, then as now, there was no doubt in anyone's mind that the place to be before, after and occasionally during the festival was the Wynkoop. I knew then that my first experience with dinner and pints at Wynkoop after the fest was certainly not to be my last.

If anything, the allure of the Wynkoop has occasionally had its draw-backs. Through my five years of GABF attendance to date, I have been late for more than one appointment because I was unable to detach myself from the warm and friendly atmosphere that so pervades the place. In fact, as I enjoyed a departing pint with *Celebrator Beer News* publisher Tom Dalldorf at the very end of that first GABF, the comfortable feel of the Wynkoop was almost responsible for me missing my flight—I arrived at the airport with but a mere ten minutes to spare!

The people at the United Airlines check in were less than pleased with me, but I didn't mind; it had been a small price to pay for one more sip of delicious Wynkoop ale.

Sauerkraut

From: Stoudt's Black Angus Restaurant
Adamstown, Pennsylvania, USA

Created by Executive Chef Chris Dunn

Speaking as someone who has long been a fan of good sauerkraut, I can honestly say that this is without question the finest example I have ever tasted. It's no wonder that it is a popular item in Stoudt's Beer Garden.

Beermate: Served with pork sausages, the natural accompaniment to this sauerkraut is Oktoberfest märzen. Not only does it maintain the German beer hall aesthetic, it tastes great, as well. Try Stoudt's own Fest or the Paulaner Oktoberfest.

Before You Begin: Juniper berries may not be the easiest ingredient to find, but the juniper flavor is very much desired in this dish. If you can't locate any berries, simply use an ounce or two of a good gin or jenever as a substitute.

2 lb sauerkraut
2 tbsp pork fat, lard or other shortening
3 medium onions, finely chopped
2 bay leaves
6 juniper berries, crushed
1 cup Oktoberfest märzen
1 tbsp caraway seeds
1 apple, peeled, cored and coarsely chopped

Place the sauerkraut in a large bowl and stir through with a fork, separating the strands and breaking up any clumps. Heat the pork fat in large skillet on medium heat and sauté the onions until translucent. Add the sauerkraut, bay leaves, juniper berries, beer, caraway seeds and apple. Simmer covered for 1 to 2 hours, adding more beer if necessary to keep the sauerkraut moist.

Serves 4 to 6.

Blackhook Baked Beans

From: The Redhook Ale Brewery and Forecasters Public House
Woodinville, Washington, USA

Created by Chefs Isles and Richard Wallace

In my last book, *A Taste for Beer*, I published a wonderful baked beans recipe from Joe Fiorito that included bacon in the ingredients. Now, in the interests of fairness, I offer a delicious vegetarian version from The Redhook Ale Brewery.

Beermate: Whether served with sausages at dinner or as part of a farmer's breakfast, baked beans call for a round but not imposing ale as an accompaniment, one with enough malt to satisfy and moderate bitterness to contrast the slow-cooked sweetness of the beans. Try a Griffon Brown Ale or Bell's Amber Ale.

Before You Begin: Because the baking heat for these beans is higher than for many recipes, and the cooking time shorter, it is important that the beans are tender from simmering before baking. And check for liquid each hour or so to make sure that they do not dry out.

1 ½ lb dried white beans
1 medium onion, diced
2 tbsp dry mustard
2/3 cup molasses
1/4 cup Worcestershire sauce
1/2 cup ketchup or chili sauce
12 oz porter

Soak the beans overnight in water. The next day, place in a large pot with fresh water on high heat. Bring to a boil, reduce heat and simmer until the beans are tender, about one hour. Drain, reserving the cooking liquid, and transfer to a bean pot or baking dish and set aside.

Add the onion, mustard, molasses, Worcestershire sauce, ketchup and porter and mix well. Add just enough of the reserved cooking liquid to cover the beans. Cover with the lid or foil and bake at 350°F for 5 to 6 hours, if necessary replenishing the lost liquid with more porter and/or bean cooking liquid. The beans are done when the ones around the edges begin to caramelize.

Serves 6 to 8 as a side dish.

Calamari

From: Great Lakes Brewing Company
Cleveland, Ohio, USA

Created by Chef Rob Ulmann

Since the calamari craze hit North America a decade or so ago, it seems as if every bar and restaurant on the continent feels compelled to serve their own interpretation, usually doing a poor job of it. Here is a great calamari to fix when you get tired of all of those other soggy, greasy versions.

Beermate: With fresh flavors of lightly sautéed vegetables coming together with the crisp and lightly seasoned calamari, I can think of no better beermate than a floral Bohemian pilsner. Try the Niagara Falls Saaz Pilsner or the firmer Czech pils, Ostravar.

Before You Begin: Frying time is of vital importance in cooking calamari; too short and the squid is raw, too long and it turns rubbery. Keep very close watch and use a quick hand when it's time to remove the rings from the oil.

1 lb squid tubes, cut into thin rings
3 cups vegetable oil
1 cup all-purpose flour
1 red pepper, julienned
1 green pepper, julienned
1 tsp minced fresh garlic
1 tsp dried parsley
Salt and pepper

In a medium sauté pan on high, heat the oil to the smoking point.

Dust the squid rings in the flour and shake off the excess. Add the rings to the hot oil and separate with tongs. Cook the squid for about 30 seconds, being careful not to move the rings around too much or else the flour will fall off.

Remove the squid from the pan and carefully pour off the oil into a receptacle. Return the pan to medium heat and add the peppers, garlic and parsley. Sauté until the peppers are tender and add the squid; salt and pepper to taste. Serve hot.

Serves 4 to 6.

GREAT LAKES BREWING COMPANY

2516 Market Street
Cleveland, Ohio, USA 44113
Phone: 216-771-2247

Since virtually the day they opened their doors in 1988, the Great Lakes Brewing Company has been a hit with Ohio beer lovers and craft-brewing industry watchers alike. Their artfully crafted and ingeniously named brews —sporting monikers like Burning River Ale, Elliot Ness Vienna Lager and Loch Erie Scotch Ale—have won favor at the Great American Beer Festival, the World Beer Championships and, of course, in the hearts of Clevelanders.

I first became acquainted with Great Lakes Brewing at the GABF of 1992, where I rated their award-winning Edmund Fitzgerald Porter quite highly and was impressed, too, by their Vienna lager. The quality of their beers certainly raised an eyebrow, as the Great Lakes region was not at that time rife with great breweries, and I made a quick mental note to remember the name for later reference.

My mental note-taking ability has never been one of my greater strengths though, and the next time I encountered the brewery was the following year at the very same event. This time it was their Burning River Ale that caught the attention of both myself and the judges, as it was awarded a silver medal in the Classic English Pale Ale category. And this time too, I promised myself that I would learn more about this small Ohio brewing company.

In the years that followed, I did, indeed, learn more. For example, I found out that Great Lakes Brewing was the first craft-brewing operation to open in Ohio and that the company had been started by two brothers, Pat and Dan Conway. Further, I discovered that their beers were distributed little outside of their home state, which accounted for the fact that I only ever seemed to hear of them when at the GABF.

Among all the information that I gathered about the Great Lakes Brewing Company, however, there was one piece of the puzzle that continued to elude me. This final revelation came as I was in the finishing stages of preparing this cookbook and needed a fine example of a Vienna lager to note as the beermate to one of the recipes. Wishing to use the Elliot Ness as that example, but needing to confirm that the brewery still produced it, I logged onto the Internet and found the Great Lakes Brewing home page. And there was that elusive detail staring me straight in the face: the Great Lakes Brewing Company was not only a brewery, it was also a brewpub!

Working faster than if I had stiff-peaked egg whites that were ready to fall, I called around and discovered that not only was the brewery a brewpub, it was a damn good one, as well, having received positive reviews from *Bon Appétit* and other respected food publications. Red-faced, I called up Pat Conway, explained my oversight and begged for recipes for this book.

To Pat's great credit, I had the recipes in hand later that same day, and not only were they prompt, they were also great! After a hastily arranged kitchen test, I knew that I had the final great North American brewpub for this book. So, as you enjoy the Great Lakes Brewing dishes, don't thank me, thank the Internet.

Stoudt's Beer Cheese Spread

From: Stoudt's Black Angus Restaurant
Adamstown, Pennsylvania, USA

Created by Executive Chef Chris Dunn

If you love cheese as I love cheese, you will relish the wonderfully vibrant and piquant flavor of this terrific spread.

Beermate: The sharpness of the taste of this dish is obviously dependent upon the cheese used, but if the cheddar has a lovely tang, the beer would have to be a firm and hoppy India pale ale such as the Anchor Liberty Ale or Bridgeport India Pale Ale.

Before You Begin: As well as being a spread, this recipe can also make a terrific cheese dip. Simply add a little extra stout until dip consistency is reached and serve it with onion crackers and large pretzels.

1 lb spreadable old cheddar
(Wispride, MacLaren's Imperial), warmed to room temperature
1 tsp minced onion
1 tbsp Worcestershire sauce
1 clove garlic, minced
Salt to taste
1½ cups dry stout

In a large mixing bowl, blend the cheese with the onion, Worcestershire, garlic and salt until smooth. Adding the beer slowly; keep blending the cheese mixture until it reaches a consistency at which it may be easily spread.

Pack the spread into a crock and refrigerate overnight.

Makes about 4 cups.

Spinnakers Baked Cheese

From: Spinnakers Brew Pub
Victoria, British Columbia, Canada

Created by George Chan and Stephen Engberf

I have always maintained that beer accompanies cheese better than does wine, and I think that this recipe proves it. Terrific as an hors d'oeuvre with crackers or served with fresh bread at lunch.

Beermate: Despite my belief that every food has a perfect beer accompaniment, I have to admit that almost any flavorful beer will complement this dish nicely. The pub goer in me, however, suggests that an English-style best bitter such as Arkell Best Bitter or the bigger Spinnakers ESB is ideal.

Before You Begin: This recipe makes a good amount of baked cheese, about six cups. If you do not need that much, simply scale the recipe back by whatever percentage you desire.

1½ lb cream cheese
1 cup butter
1 cup sour cream
1 cup grated asiago cheese
1 cup finely chopped or crumbled white cheddar
1/2 cup diced fresh mushrooms
1/2 cup diced sun-dried tomatoes
1/4 cup chopped chives
2 cloves garlic, crushed and minced
2 tbsp paprika

In a large bowl or food processor, blend together all of the ingredients. Place in one or more ceramic bowls and heat in a 350°F oven until the top is golden and the cheese is hot. Serve with crackers for dipping or your favorite fresh bread. It will keep for up to one week if tightly covered and refrigerated.

Makes approximately 6 cups.

SPINNAKERS BREW PUB
2308 Catherine Street
Victoria, British Columbia, Canada V9A 3S8
Phone: 250-384-0332

Back in 1982, a man by the name of John Mitchell built the very first modern brewpub in North America, an operation called the Horseshoe Bay Brewing Company located at the Horseshoe Bay ferry terminal near Vancouver, British Columbia. The only catch to this pioneer operation was that owing to the odd legislative requirements that existed in those early days of the craft-brewing renaissance, the pub and the brewery were not housed in the same building, with the brewery being located a short distance away from the restaurant and pub. Make no mistake about it though, Horseshoe Bay Brewing was very much a brewpub.

The incongruity of brewery and pub being separate entities must have eaten at Mitchell, however, because it was only a short time after Horseshoe Bay opened that he split from the ownership group and undertook to create Canada's first brewpub with an in-house brewery. That new operation was Spinnakers Brew Pub in Victoria, British Columbia.

Located just a few minutes from the downtown of what is arguably Canada's most authentically British city, Spinnakers opened in 1984 as a very British-style pub. The atmosphere was, and is, casual and relaxed, the fare owed a great deal to classic British pub cuisine and customers had to order and retrieve their beer and food from the bar, just as they would were they in a pub in the UK. Local reaction was swift and positive and Spinnakers was an immediate hit.

My first visit to Spinnakers came in the late 1980s and the attraction was immediate. Here was a place without pretence or even formality, but also one that had character to spare. The ales were very fine, the food delicious and the overall feel of the place one of extreme comfort. As I said then, and have repeated many times since, the existence of Spinnakers was almost enough to make me want to move to Victoria.

When I later returned to Spinnakers in the spring of 1993, changes had taken place. Renovations had moved the pub up to the second floor of the lodge-style building and a full-service, main-floor dining room had been added to the mix. To my relief, however, the important aspects of the brew-pub — the food, the beer, the atmosphere — had remained wonderfully the same.

In the years since Spinnakers first opened its doors, it has become a institution. For years it stood as unquestionably the finest brewpub in Western Canada and even today, although it has been joined by many other fine British Columbian brewpubs, it still holds a place of honor and respect within the brewing industry. Testament to the fact that sometimes first and finest really can go together.

Artichoke Crock

From: Great Lakes Brewing Company
Cleveland, Ohio, USA

Created by Chef Rob Ulmann

Artichokes often intimidate amateur chefs, but the canned or jarred marinated hearts couldn't be easier to work with and are very useful in baked dishes such as this one. And as you can see from the directions below, the preparation is anything but intimidating.

Beermate: Remembering that the artichokes will sweeten the flavor of the beer you enjoy with this delicious appetizer and bearing in mind that real Parmesan cheese has quite a bite, I would suggest an extra special bitter as a perfect accompaniment. Try an Equinox ESB or a Shaftebury ESB.

Before You Begin: The better the cheese you use in this dish, the better the taste will be. Throw out your old tins of grated plastic and buy a block of real Parmesan like Parmigiano Reggiano or Grana Padano.

Two 12-oz jars artichoke hearts (drained and quartered)
1 small red pepper, diced
1½ cups grated Parmesan cheese
1 cup mayonnaise
1/2 cup banana pepper rings
1 tbsp chopped garlic
1 tsp hot pepper flakes
Pinch cayenne pepper

In a large bowl, mix together all of the ingredients. Divide the mixture evenly between two 16-oz ovenproof dishes. Bake in a 350°F oven for 25 minutes or until golden brown.

Makes approximately 4 cups.

English Stilton Tart

From: Dock Street Brewing Company
Philadelphia, Pennsylvania, USA

Created by Chefs Richard Barlow and Barbara Contino

Savory tarts are an important part of English pub fare and this New World example would definitely be at home in any British country pub.

Beermate: Being classic pub grub, it should come as no surprise that the best accompaniment to this tart is the classic British pub ale: best bitter. Try a Belk's Extra Special Bitter or Thomas Hardy's Country Bitter.

Before You Begin: This recipe can be easily modified to make individual tartlettes instead of one large tart; just remember to adjust the cooking times accordingly. The pastry also freezes very well if you wish to make it ahead of time.

For the Tart Pastry:
2/3 cup butter
2 cups all-purpose flour
1/2 cup whole wheat flour
1 tsp ground coriander
1 tsp kosher salt
1/4 tsp black pepper
1/4 tsp mace
1/8 tsp cayenne
Ice water (as needed)

For the Filling:
4 cups washed and diced leeks
1½ peeled, cored and diced apples
Butter as needed
1½ cups heavy cream
3 eggs
1/2 tsp salt
1/4 tsp nutmeg
1/4 tsp cayenne
1/4 tsp pepper
Pinch of mace
1½ cups crumbled Stilton cheese

To make the pastry, first dice the butter and return it to refrigerator. In a large bowl, combine the flours, coriander, salt and pepper, mace and cayenne. With 2 knives or a pastry cutter, cut the butter into the dough until it resembles a fine meal. Adding 1 tsp of ice water at a time, knead the dough until it forms a ball. Refrigerate for at least 30 minutes or until ready to use.

When ready to make the tart, bring the pastry to room temperature and roll out the dough. Fit the dough into 9-inch pie plate, prick the bottom all over with a fork, line with parchment paper and pie weights or dry beans and bake in a 375°F oven for 25 minutes. Remove the weights and parchment and bake further at 325°F for 20 minutes. Let cool.

In a large pan on medium heat, sauté the leeks and apples in butter until they are fully cooked but the apples remain firm. Let cool.

In a large mixing bowl, whisk together the cream, eggs, salt, nutmeg, cayenne, pepper and mace. Line the baked tart shell with half of the apples and leeks and cover with the crumbled Stilton. Top with the rest of the apples and leeks, pour in the custard and bake in a 350°F oven for about 1 hour or until done.

Serves 4 to 8.

DOCK STREET BREWING COMPANY
2 Logan Square
Philadelphia, Pennsylvania, USA 19103
Phone: 215-496-0413

It was while I was in Philadelphia en route to a historic tasting of eight vintages of Thomas Hardy's Ale that I was first introduced to the Dock Street Brewing Company. At a time when there were all too few truly great brewpubs in the northeastern United States, it struck me almost immediately that I had found a classic.

The two gentlemen who handled the introduction were Andy Musser, the veteran commentator for the Philadelphia Phillies, whom I had met in San Francisco sometime earlier, and Ben Myers, then a Philadelphia-based beer writer and now the communications director for Pyramid Brewing of Seattle. I could scarcely have asked for better beer guides, as they both dutifully set about acquainting me with everything beer-related in the City of Brotherly Love.

Our first stop was Dock Street, a city-center brewery restaurant that was, and is, by far Philadelphia's best-known brewpub and in which Andy admitted to owning a few minor shares. There was little need for him to try to embellish the quality of the operation. I knew I had hit upon something special as soon as I laid eyes on the list of beers brewed at this brewery restaurant. In total, there were 32 different styles listed on that sheet, each available as space and seasonal demand dictated, and as Dock Street's accomplished brewer Nick Funnell explained, others were being developed all the time.

This kind of diversity often tends to wear thin a brewer's expertise, but such was not the case at Dock Street. Each of the eight beers I sampled that night was well-constructed and flavorful, and most importantly, not one tasted like it had been rushed or haphazardly brewed out of a sense of duty rather than devotion. From the first sip, it was obvious that Nick was serious about his beer.

So serious, in fact, that he had even gone so far as to forge a link between Philadelphia's colonial past and brewpub present by producing a beer according to a recipe purported to be Thomas Jefferson's own formulation. The beer, Thomas Jefferson Ale, better known as TJ, was potent at almost 9% alcohol by volume, intensely fruity and blessed with one of the most bourbon-like finishes I have ever noted in a beer. If this ale was meant to be a novelty, it was a most extraordinary one, indeed.

Sitting around the last vestiges of our dinners that night, sipping ever so slowly from our ebbing glasses of TJ, Andy, Ben, Nick and I must have spent a good 20 minutes discussing that one fine ale. And I imagine that we could have very easily sat and conversed for hours longer had not the siren's call of our brewpub and beer-bar tour schedule taken us away to our next stop. Which was really a pity, because as enjoyable as the remainder of the evening was, I can't help but think that staying at Dock Street might have been even more pleasurable.

Gila Monster Eggs

From: Globe Brewery & Barbecue Co.
Globe, Arizona, USA

Created by Candy Schermerhorn

Cousins to the Armadillo Eggs of Texas and Mexican Mice, these cheese-stuffed jalapeños add an Arizona crunch with a coating of crushed tortilla chips.

Beermate: These "eggs" pack a punch and that means that a fair amount of hoppiness is desired in a beermate. Try a chilled India pale ale like the Fish Eye IPA or the Brooklyn East India Pale Ale.

Before You Begin: Take your time frying and keep the cooked jalapeños warm in the oven if necessary.

8 oz cream cheese
1/2 cup grated Monterey Jack cheese
1 large shallot, peeled and quartered
1/2 tsp coriander seed, toasted and ground
1/2 tsp cumin seed, toasted and ground
24 large fresh jalapeño peppers, split and seeded
Flour as needed, for coating the peppers
1/2 cup Amber Ale
2/3 cup all-purpose flour
2 egg whites
1/2 tsp liquid smoke, mesquite if possible
1/2 tsp each salt and ground pepper
2 cups finely crushed tortilla chips
Oil for frying

In a food processor or in a large bowl working with a whisk, blend the cream cheese, Monterey Jack cheese, shallot, ground coriander and cumin seed until smooth. Generously mound the mixture inside each jalapeño half.

Roll each stuffed jalapeño half in flour and shake off any excess. Set jalapeños aside. Whisk together the ale, flour, egg whites, liquid smoke, salt and pepper in a bowl.

Heat the oil for frying to 375°F. When the oil is hot, dip the floured jalapeños into the beer batter and roll in the crushed chips. Working in batches, gently dunk the coated jalapeños into the hot oil and fry until golden brown. Remove the jalapeños from the oil and drain on paper towels. Serve while hot.

Makes 48.

SOUPS

Lancashire Soup

From: Bushwakker Brewing Company
Regina, Saskatchewan, Canada

Created by Chef Mike Monette

A creamy, warming and filling soup for a cold winter's day.

Beermate: Because old cheddar is the main flavor ingredient in this soup, it is best served with one of the cheese's two natural beer accompaniments: British-style pale ale or best bitter. And given the creaminess of the soup, I'm inclined to choose a pale ale like Hart Amber Ale or Samuel Smith Pale Ale.

Before You Begin: Make sure that your milk is hot before you begin adding it to the soup, or else it may curdle. And if you are feeling extravagant, substitute true Lancashire cheese for the cheddar and mozzarella mix for an even better soup.

10 cups milk
2½ cups butter
1 small onion, finely diced
2 cups all-purpose flour
5 cups pale ale
Pinch dried oregano
Pinch dried basil
Pinch dried thyme
Salt and pepper to taste
1½ cups grated mixed old white cheddar and mozzarella
Whipped cream and parsley for garnish

Pour the milk into a pot and place on a back burner on medium-low heat, being careful to watch that it does not burn. In a separate large pot on low heat, melt the butter and sauté the onion until tender. Slowly add the flour to form a roux. Continue cooking the roux until it reaches a tan color. Add the pale ale a cup at a time, stirring constantly and breaking up any lumps that may form. Slowly add the hot milk, stirring constantly. Allow the soup to simmer on low heat for 20 to 30 minutes.

Before serving, add the oregano, basil, thyme and salt and pepper. Add the grated cheese and stir until all of the cheese has melted. Serve in soup plates with a dollop of whipped cream in the center and sprinkled with parsley.

Makes 4 to 5 quarts of soup.

BUSHWAKKER BREWING COMPANY

2206 Dewdney Avenue
Regina, Saskatchewan, Canada S4R 1H3
Phone: 306-359-7276

One runs into many busy people when covering the beer industry. There are those in this business I know only from meetings in hotel lobbies during check in or check out times and others I habitually (or so it seems) bump into at airports. There are people like "Wicked" Pete Slosberg who spend months every year crisscrossing the continent and others who always seem to be in the middle of running from one place to another. And then there is Bev Robertson, who makes us all look lazy.

The owner of the successful Bushwakker Brewing Company brewpub in Regina, Saskatchewan, Bev is a man who wears many hats. When he started the Bushwakker, he was a brewpub brewer, award-winning homebrewer, brewpub manager and university professor. A few years later when I first met him, he was still a university professor and brewpub manager, but had handed most of the brewing chores at Bushwakker over to his son, Scott. This is not to say that Bev was slowing down though, because he had added working on a brewpub franchise partnership in nearby Winnipeg, Manitoba, to the list of things on his plate. Oh, and did I mention his work for the university alumni association?

In another place run by another individual, all of this activity might mean that the establishment would suffer from absentee ownership, a killer disease in the service trade. But not so at the Bushwakker. Every single time I have visited Regina, I have been impressed by the high quality of the beer, food and service at the Bushwakker. In fact, I can't think of a single place in the province of Saskatchewan where I would rather sit down for a beer.

Just how impressive the Bushwakker really was struck home as I was having dinner with a fellow beer writer during the 1996 Great American Beer Festival. With his being a Colorado resident, I expected that when my colleague jokingly complained about my not writing enough about his favorite brewery, he was talking about one of that state's many fine brewpubs. But no, the pub he was referring to was the Bushwakker, located some 800 miles north of Denver!

When I last saw the man responsible for creating such lasting, long-distance impressions, Bev Robertson had become part owner of a Regina restaurant, and was contemplating keg sales of Bushwakker beer to other local licensees and even a possible entry into the retail market. In addition, the Winnipeg brewpub was still a going concern and he had been doing some brewery consulting work in China, while sizing up the possibilities there, as well.

Although he did admit to me that he is taking retirement from the university in the not-too-distant future, I somehow doubt that it will slow him down too much. After all, once he has Saskatchewan, Manitoba and parts of China under wraps, there is always the United States. I know he has one customer waiting for him in Colorado.

Cheddar Vegetable Soup

From: The Granite Brewery
Toronto, Ontario, Canada

Created by Chef Clark Nickerson

This soup allows the flavor of the cheddar to shine through.

Beermate: I'd suggest a malty Scottish-style ale such as McTarnahans Ale or St. Andrew's Ale to provide a counterpoint to the cheese and the pale ale's hoppiness.

Before You Begin: Because the beer goes in at the end of this recipe, it is best not to use too hoppy a pale ale; stick to British-style examples such as the Pike Pale Ale or Bass. Also, be sure to allow the mixture to cool after adding the cream and before putting in the ale and cheese. This ensures that your soup will not curdle.

1 small onion, minced
1 carrot, diced
1 stalk celery, chopped
1/4 cup butter
1/4 cup all-purpose flour
1/2 tsp each dry mustard and paprika
Pinch nutmeg
1/4 bunch each broccoli and cauliflower, chopped (optional)
4 cups chicken broth
1 cup 10% table cream
1 cup grated old Canadian cheddar
1 cup pale ale
chopped parsley

In a large pot over medium heat, sauté the onion, carrot and celery in the butter until the carrots are tender, stirring occasionally. Slowly add the flour to form a roux and remove the pot from the heat.

Add the dry mustard, paprika and nutmeg and mix well. Add the broccoli and cauliflower, if desired. Gradually add the chicken broth while stirring, breaking up any lumps that may form.

Return to the burner on low heat and cook for approximately 20 minutes, stirring occasionally. Remove the pot from the heat again to stir in the cream. Allow to cool for 5 minutes, then add the cheddar and beer and return the pot to the burner. Stir over low heat until the cheddar melts and serve topped with a bit more grated cheddar, if desired, and a sprinkling of parsley.

Serves 6.

Carrot Lager Soup

From: The Kingston Brewing Company
Kingston, Ontario, Canada

Created by Chef Roger Holmes

This is a classic "day-old" soup, meaning that it is at its best when prepared the day before it is to be served. This trait, combined with the amount that this recipe yields, makes it an ideal dish for fall or winter entertaining.

Beermate: Despite the size of the recipe relative to the size of the ginger, curry powder and Worcestershire sauce quantities, this soup has a very nice spiciness to it. With this in mind, I'd recommend a chilled India pale ale, something like the Blind Pig IPA or the Brooklyn East India Pale Ale perhaps.

Before You Begin: When making the roux on top of the vegetables, take your time and add the flour gradually, making sure that it is well incorporated before adding more. Likewise, add the lager and the stock slowly so that you don't end up with lumps in your soup.

1/2 lb butter
8 large carrots, peeled and grated
1 onion, peeled and grated
1 thumb-sized piece ginger, peeled and grated
5 cloves garlic, minced
1/2 cup all-purpose flour
2 cups lager
10 cups chicken stock
1 cinnamon stick
1 tbsp curry powder
Salt and pepper to taste
5 dashes Worcestershire sauce
1/2 cup heavy cream

Melt the butter in a large pot over low heat. Add the carrots, onion, ginger and garlic and sauté until the vegetables are cooked. Slowly incorporate the flour to form a roux and cook for another 10 minutes, stirring constantly. Slowly add the lager and mix well. Slowly add the chicken stock, being careful to break down any lumps that may form. Simmer the soup for 1 hour.

Add the cinnamon stick, curry powder, salt and pepper, Worcestershire sauce and cream. Mix thoroughly. If possible, allow soup to rest overnight before serving.

Serves 12 to 14.

Roasted Butternut Squash and Beer Soup

From: C'est What Brewery, Winery and Restaurant
Toronto, Ontario, Canada

Created by Jeff Sararas

The recipe for this great winter soup calls for butternut squash, but I would guess that it would work equally well with most winter squash varieties.

Beermate: This is a fairly mild soup. As such, I'm inclined to offer it the contrasting flavor of a pumpkin spice beer like Buffalo Bill's Pumpkin Ale or a spiced Belgian ale such as La Chouffe.

Before You Begin: Don't panic when the skins of the squash turn brown and begin to blister when you are baking them; that's supposed to happen!

2 large butternut squash, halved lengthwise and seeded
4 small yams, washed
1 onion, loose skin removed but not peeled
1 whole bulb garlic, loose skin removed but not peeled
Water
2 tbsp dried thyme
Salt, pepper and cayenne to taste
1 tbsp Dijon mustard
1 cup gueuze
3/4 cup grated old cheddar

Rub the cut surfaces of the squash and all of the yams, onion and garlic with vegetable oil. Place the squash cut sides down on a large baking sheet, along with the yams, onion and garlic, and place on the middle rack of an oven preheated to 450°F. Let bake for about 1 hour or until the necks of the squash are tender enough to be easily pricked with a knife. Set aside to cool.

When the vegetables are cool enough to handle, peel the yams and onion and cut them into chunks. Slice off the root end of the garlic before separating it into cloves, then squeeze the roasted garlic out of each clove. Scoop the flesh out of the squash skins and combine it with the garlic, yams and onion. Purée all of this in batches and transfer to a large soup pot, adding just enough water to make it easy to stir. Bring the vegetable mixture to a simmer and add thyme, salt, pepper and cayenne. In a small bowl, combine the Dijon mustard with 1/2 cup of the soup, mix well and return it all to pot. Add the beer and simmer for 10 to 15 minutes longer. Taste and adjust seasonings as desired.

Just prior to serving, stir in the cheddar, reserving 1/4 cup to garnish.
Serves 4 to 6.

¿C'EST WHAT?
BREWERY - WINERY- RESTAURANT

C'EST WHAT BREWERY, WINERY AND RESTAURANT
67 Front Street East
Toronto, Ontario, Canada M5E 1B5
Phone: 416-867-9791

The mid-1980s craze for craft-brewed beer hit southern Ontario fairly early, relative to many, if not most, other parts of North America. The province's first microbrewery, Brick Brewing in Waterloo, opened in 1984 and it was quickly followed by two others. Not long after that, the first pair of brew-pubs opened and the craft-beer renaissance in Ontario was in full swing.

Even so, it was not until the early years of the 1990s that modern beer-related notoriety really hit Ontario, as the province became a hotbed of what has come to be known as brew-on-premises, or BOP, brewing. The idea behind the BOP was that people could come to a shop that was set up with several small brew kettles and brew their own beer without having to deal with the fuss-and-muss of brewing at home. Although the concept originated in British Columbia, it was in Ontario that it really took off.

While the explosive popularity of BOPing died down after only a couple of years, it did leave in its wake a curious brewpub-related phenomenon known as the ferment-pub. Legal under a quirk of Ontario's brewpub leg-islation, a ferment-pub is a bar or restaurant that contracts a BOP to produce unfermented beer (called wort) for them and ferments it on their own premises. In this fashion, the bar gets its own unique, house-label beers without having to go to the trouble of installing a full brewery or con-tracting a large production run to a craft brewery. As a business plan goes, it is ingenious.

As a brewing scheme, however, the ferment-pub has for the most part flopped. With few exceptions, the ferment-pubs of Ontario have produced uninteresting brews with little to recommend them. *With a few exceptions.*

The biggest one is the Toronto beer bar and ferment-pub known as C'est What. With what must be considered remarkable consistency, given the circumstances, C'est What continually turns out good to excellent ales from their backroom "fermentery." From their cask-conditioned Mild Brown

Ale to such eclectic specialties as a saison-style ale, C'est What has impressed since almost the first day they began the process. Such has been their success that they have even become known for their flagship Coffee Porter, brewed with fresh coffee beans, which is now bottled for them by the local craft brewery, Trafalgar Brewing.

In retrospect, it is easy to figure that good ales might have been expected from C'est What. Back in 1988, they were the first bona fide beer bar to set up in Toronto and the bar was still very young when they introduced their practice of offering only craft-brewed beers for sale on the premises. Even today, C'est What remains one of the best, if not the best, beer destination in Toronto, offering outstanding, reasonably priced food, live entertainment seven nights a week and 26 taps dedicated to the ales and lagers of the craft breweries of Ontario. Including, of course, a few of their very own.

Irish Potato and Bacon Soup

From: Hale's Ales Brewery, Ltd.
Seattle, Washington, USA

Created by Chef Doug Courter

They developed this soup at Hale's a few years ago for their St. Patrick's Day celebrations and quickly found that it was just too popular to serve but once a year.

Beermate: Being an Irish soup, there is really only one kind of beer that can be served alongside it — dry Irish stout. Fortunately, a pint of Guinness or Sierra Nevada Stout makes for a great complement.

1/2 lb sliced bacon, diced

1/2 lb (2-3) onions, diced

1/2 lb green cabbage, shredded

1/4 tsp nutmeg

1/4 tsp thyme leaves

2 whole bay leaves

3 cups Irish ale

2 lb (5-6 medium-sized) potatoes, peeled and cut into bite-size pieces

4 cups milk

2 tsp salt

1 tsp black pepper

In a large, heavy-bottomed pot, cook the bacon until lightly browned. Drain off all but 2 tbsp of the fat and add the onions, cabbage, nutmeg, thyme and bay leaves. Cook until the cabbage and onions are well wilted and fragrant. Add the ale and potatoes along with half the milk. Bring the soup to a boil, reduce heat and simmer, strirring well to break up the potatoes. Add milk as needed to thin the soup and prevent it from scorching.

Continue simmering the soup for an hour or more if needed, stirring occasionally. If necessary, add milk as needed to prevent the soup from becoming too thick. Season with salt and pepper before serving.

Serves 6 to 8.

Spicy Beef Watermelon Ale Soup

From: Spinnakers Brew Pub
Victoria, British Columbia, Canada

Created by Chefs George Chan and Stephen Engberf

As unorthodox as this recipe may be, when all of the divergent flavors blend together the result is a spicy, satisfying soup.

Beermate: The watermelon brings a hint of sweetness to the spice in this dish and so mellows the heat effect of the chili powder, ginger and jalapeño. As a result, a German-style alt beer is a very satisfying partner to this dish, with enough body to balance the beef, a moderate hoppiness to contrast the spice and an overall lightness that truly complements the soup. Try a Bolten Alt or Alaskan Amber Alt-Style Beer.

Before You Begin: Homemade defatted chicken or beef stock is the best for this or any dish, but making it yourself is not always practical. Fortunately, good canned stocks do exist and will work as able substitutes.

> 8 oz minced beef sirloin
> 1 small red onion, finely chopped
> 1 small piece ginger, finely chopped
> 1 tbsp minced garlic
> 3 lb (6 cups puréed) seedless watermelon
> 2 tbsp tomato paste
> 2 tbsp chili powder
> Pinch dried thyme
> Pinch dried basil
> Pinch cinnamon
> 1 tsp minced fresh jalapeño
> 1 tbsp brown sugar
> 8 cups chicken or beef stock
> 2 cups dark ale
> Pinch black pepper
> 1 tbsp salt or to taste

In a large pot, cook the beef well over medium heat. Drain and add the onion, ginger and garlic. Cook until the onion becomes tender and then add the watermelon, tomato paste, chili powder, thyme, basil, cinnamon, jalapeño, sugar, stock, ale and salt and pepper. Bring to a boil and reduce the heat to low, stirring occasionally. Continue to simmer for 20 minutes, thickening with flour or cornstarch if desired.

Serves 6.

Pumpkin and Stout Soup

From: Pepperwood Bistro
Burlington, Ontario, Canada

Created by Chef Alex Mickalow

This rich and flavorful soup is uncommonly easy to make and a delight on a chilly fall day. Served with some good, honest bread, it makes for a hearty meal at any time of the day.

Beermate: I can't help it; when I think of pumpkin, I think of pumpkin pie spices like allspice, nutmeg, cinnamon and ginger. So when I serve this soup, I automatically reach for a pumpkin spice beer like the Lakefront Pumpkin Lager or the Adlerbrau Pumpkin Spice.

Before You Begin: It is important not to boil this soup or else the aromatics of the beer will be lost. And if you wish to follow Chef Alex's suggestion, you will add a lot more than a pinch of ginger — he says that it reminds him of Thanksgiving dinner!

1 onion, finely diced
1 lb (2-3 medium) potatoes, peeled and diced
1/4 cup butter
1½ cups stout or porter
4 cups vegetable stock
2 cups pumpkin purée (canned is fine)
Pinch salt and pepper
Pinch ground ginger and cinnamon

In a large pot on medium heat, sauté the onions and potatoes in butter until the onions are translucent. Add the stout and simmer for 10 minutes. Add the vegetable stock, pumpkin, salt, pepper, ginger and cinnamon and continue to simmer until the potatoes are soft. Purée the soup and adjust the seasonings to taste.

Serves 6.

PEPPERWOOD BISTRO
1455 Lakeshore Road
Burlington, Ontario, Canada L7S 1B5
Phone: 416-333-6999

As anyone from the brewing industry will tell you, brewing equipment is extremely recyclable. Old breweries are quickly stripped down and sold off in parts, to take their place in new breweries until inevitably, one or two of these fall by the wayside and send the equipment on to its next brewing stop. Indeed, in these times of enormous growth in the craft-brewing sector, it is rare to enter a brewery and not find remnants of a prior, failed enterprise.

Brewery locations, however, are not normally quite so reusable. Whether it comes as a result of superstition or chance, it is uncommon to find the premises of a failed brewery or brewpub again functioning in the form of its original intent. Most brewpubs simply go on to become nonbrewing clubs, bars or restaurants.

This was not the case with one notable location in Burlington, Ontario, a city-suburb of Hamilton located less than an hour's drive from Toronto. It was there that an inauspicious brewpub known by the rather undignified name of Suds International first found a home on the main boulevard by the shores of Lake Ontario. It was a malt extract operation, as were many of the province's early brewpubs, and it did not last long. Its space, however, lived on as a brewpub.

The second time around, the brewing tenant was a Luxembourg brewpub, part of an ill-fated chain of franchised brewpub operations that sprang up in Ontario and Saskatchewan in the early part of the 1990s and faded away almost as quickly. The Burlington Luxembourg eventually suffered the same fate as the other members of the chain and the space grew once again empty.

When I heard that a third brewpub was planning on taking a crack at the same premises, I feared for the new owners. If once was a warning, surely twice was a neon sign screaming "Just Don't Do It!" But then again, I didn't know Mike Dine.

Mike is the force behind the Pepperwood Bistro and, as I found upon my first visit to the new brewpub, is also a man of vision. The prior failing of the space had been its warehouse ambience — not exactly a cosy atmosphere for relaxed beer enjoyment — so to counter that, Mike had the area broken down into small, sub-spaces using innovative dividers and enclosures. Further, he had "lowered" the ceiling with the skilled use of decoration and, almost impossibly, given this cavernous expanse a real feeling of ... well, intimacy.

Mike had also seen what so many Ontario brewpub owners and managers had not, which was that fine ales and great food naturally went together. Above all, I believe that this is the reason that Burlington residents and visitors alike continue to return to the Pepperwood, and I know that it is the reason I make a point to stop by whenever I am in the neighborhood. It is also why the Pepperwood Bistro is going strong in a spot that had previously claimed two brewpubs.

Chicken and Sausage Gumbo

From: Denison's Brewing Company & Restaurants
Toronto, Ontario, Canada

Created by Chef Glenroy Anderson

A rich and satisfying take on a Cajun mainstay and proof that great gumbos can be created outside of Louisiana.

Beermate: Although Chef Anderson's gumbo is spicy, it is at least equally herbal and nutty, making the choice of a companion beer a tough one. I think that a contrast is appropriate here, in the form of a malty dark lager like the König Ludwig Dunkel or Hermann's Bavarian Dark Lager.

Before You Begin: The roux is a main flavor ingredient in this and any proper gumbo. Make sure that you cook it slowly until it is deep brown and nutty to the taste. If you wish, you can make your roux ahead of time and store it in the refrigerator for up to a week.

1 cup vegetable oil
1 cup all-purpose flour
2 stalks celery
1/2 cup red pepper, diced
1/2 cup green pepper, diced
1/2 cup onion, diced
1/2 cup okra, chopped
1 jalapeño, minced
2 tsp paprika
1 tbsp cayenne pepper
1 tbsp dried basil
2 tsp dried oregano
2 tsp dried thyme
1 small bay leaf
1/2 tbsp cracked black peppercorns
2 tsp crushed dried chilies
1 tbsp minced garlic
8 cups chicken stock
1 lb boneless chicken breasts
1 lb pork sausages

In a large, heavy-bottomed pot, heat the oil on medium until very hot and add the flour. Quickly whisk the flour and oil until it is fully incorporated and then continue cooking on medium until it becomes dark brown, stirring constantly with a wooden spoon. This process should take about 20 to 25 minutes.

When the roux is made, add all of the vegetables and herbs and stir until well mixed. Slowly add the chicken stock, stirring constantly and breaking up any lumps that may form with the back of the wooden spoon. When all of the stock has been added, bring the gumbo to a boil and reduce to simmer. Let simmer for 1 hour and adjust the seasonings to taste. Remove from heat and let sit overnight in the refrigerator if possible.

Prior to serving, broil or grill the sausage and chicken until done. Cut into bite-size pieces and add to the gumbo while it warms. Let simmer for 10 to 15 minutes before serving.

Serves 6 to 8.

DENISON'S BREWING COMPANY

DENISON'S BREWING COMPANY & RESTAURANTS
75 Victoria Street
Toronto, Ontario, Canada M5C 2B1
Phone: 416-360-5877

I do not know for certain, but I would be willing to bet that there are few North American brewpubs that can boast a prince among their owners. And even if they can, I would lay long odds that they can't also brag that a member of one of the continent's most famous brewing families is one of their investors. Denison's Brewing Company of Toronto can lay claim to both.

The prince in question is Prince Luitpold of Bavaria, owner of Germany's Kaltenberg Brewery, located just outside of Munich, and the manner in which he got involved with Denison's has its origins in his 1984 meeting with a member of Canada's brewing "nobility," Eric Molson. The two men had met with members of the American brewery Coors to discuss the possibility of establishing a joint distribution network in the US. Although that deal did not work out, the prince's interest in the North American market had been piqued.

By early 1987, the prince had finally assured himself of a brewing toe-hold on the continent through a partnership with, among others, Eric Molson, to open Toronto's first, and to date only, lager-only brewpub, Denison's. Organization and construction on the downtown site was slow, but the brew-pub eventually opened its doors in the fall of 1989 and began serving its flagship Royal Dunkel and both filtered and unfiltered versions of its lager.

Brewer Michael Hancock, a former Molson employee and a partner in the new enterprise, soon found that there was a market for the occasional specialty beer at Denison's and began producing several seasonal varieties. So far, these have included a highly flavorful Bock and the very smooth and moderately hoppy Märzen, along with perhaps his best-known and critically lauded beer, a summer Weizen fermented with the somewhat unpredictable, but always interesting, wheat beer yeast of Kaltenberg.

It was because of that same wheat beer yeast, in fact, that Michael Hancock and I first became acquainted. Writing in *The Toronto Star* during the summer of 1992, I had commented that Denison's Weizen appeared to have an unintentionally high level of banana character typically associated with the use of an authentic Bavarian Weizen yeast, an impression I had formed through a conversation with Michael and, of course, a tasting of the beer. My impression, as Michael saw it, had been incorrect and he was soon on the phone with me explaining his satisfaction with the degree of banana esters in his Weizen. A long conversation ensued, a clarification was published two weeks later and the Weizen has since become my favorite of Denison's several fine brews.

Since that time, I have enjoyed many beers with Michael and found his pride in his craftsmanship and his support for the craft-beer industry as a whole to be unsurpassed by anyone in the business. As for the prince, I think he may still be a little miffed over my comments about his yeast.

Ale-Spiked Smoked Salmon Chowder

From: McMenamins Edgefield Estate
The Black Rabbit Restaurant
Troutdale, Oregon, USA

Created by Chef Geri Marz

This almost sinfully rich chowder gets a very pleasant smoky taste from the salmon. Flag this recipe for making on the next Robbie Burns' Day.

Beermate: This soup is flavorful enough that it can stand its ground against almost any beverage pairing, and is actually quite delicious when served with a good single malt Islay whiskey. In the beer realm, I'd suggest a Scotch ale such as the Douglas Scotch Ale or a strong old ale such as the Hair of the Dog Adambier.

Before You Begin: Watch your beer selection on this one; too hoppy an ale will make a mess of your chowder. Select a malty ale for this recipe, even a strong one if you wish.

5 oz (5-6 slices) bacon
2 stalks celery, diced
1 medium onion, diced
1 tbsp chopped garlic
1 tbsp chopped shallots
3 cups brown ale
5 cups clam stock
6½ cups heavy cream
1 tsp dried dill
1 bay leaf
Salt and pepper to taste
Cornstarch for thickening (as needed)
1 lb smoked salmon, thinly sliced

In a large pot on medium heat, cook the bacon until crisp. Drain off only excess fat and add celery, onion, garlic and shallots. Sauté the vegetables until soft and deglaze the pot with the beer. Reduce beer by half.

Add the clam stock, cream and dill, bay leaf, and salt and pepper to the pot and mix well. Bring the soup to a simmer. In a cup, add cold water to a small amount of cornstarch and mix until it has completely disolved. Add this to the soup and stir. Repeat as needed until the soup has thickened. Add smoked salmon and adjust seasonings to taste.

Serves 10 to 12.

EDGEFIELD

McMENAMINS EDGEFIELD ESTATE
THE BLACK RABBIT RESTAURANT

2126 S.W. Halsey
Troutdale, Oregon, USA 97060
Phone: 503-669-8610

Picture a large country estate resort. Now add a fine dining restaurant and a brewpub. Next, throw in a full-service movie theatre where you can enjoy a draught ale and a sandwich while you watch a flick. Then latch on a winery and wine bar and the Pacific northwest's smallest sports bar. Now top it all off with a golf course.

The newest Sheraton showcase perhaps, or a cutting-edge Four Seasons resort? No, it's McMenamins Edgefield Estate and it is about the most unusual getaway resort you will ever find.

Brothers Mike and Brian McMenamin are known as Portland's brewpub kings, which is no small feat in a city that boasts more breweries per capita than any other in North America! And Edgefield is their crowning glory, which is also no small feat considering that the brothers own and operate more than 30 brewpubs, pubs and theatre pubs in Oregon and Washington state. It is a resort that is as eclectic as are the brothers themselves.

My visit to Edgefield came in the spring of 1996 during a northwestern swing that took me to Vancouver, Seattle, Portland, Newport and Troutdale, Oregon. It was in the last locale that I spent a night at Edgefield. My stay began with a tour of the facilities, a treat that is regularly offered to all guests, not just media types. I saw all of the amenities, including the on-site brewery and winery, and was introduced to all of the beautiful oddities of Edgefield. Perhaps the most unusual aspect of the place were the murals that covered most of the hallways in the hotel, each one painted by a different artist bound only to continue the theme developed by the previous painter. Had I been less tired, hungry and thirsty, it would have been very easy to spend an hour or two just following the progress of the walls.

As impressed as I was with the surroundings at Edgefield—I still long to return and take photos—I worried that such esotericism might preclude a dedication to the gastronomic arts, as is often the case when aesthetics are given priority in bars, restaurants and, yes, even hotels and resorts. In this case, however, my fears were completely unfounded. Dinner that night at the Black Rabbit Restaurant proved to be not only delicious, but also most reasonably priced.

When I left Edgefield the next day, I already felt as if I was leaving the house of a good friend. For even with all of its size and unconventional decoration, Edgefield does possess those qualities most sought after in any hotel: a sense of comfort and homeyness.

SALADS

Red Tail Pasta Salad   62

Rotisserie Chicken Salad   63

Grilled Shrimp Salad   64

Scallop Seviche   65

Mesclun Greens with Baked Pecan-Crusted Goat
Cheese and Caramelized Apple-Shallot Vinaigrette   66

Salad of Seasonal Wild Greens,
Smoked Long Island Duckling and
Lindemans Peche Lambic Vinaigrette   69

Grilled Chicken with Pears, Dried Cherries
and Toasted Walnuts with Pear Vinaigrette   72

Red Tail Pasta Salad

From: The Mendocino Brewing Company
Hopland, California, USA

Created by Chef Vicki Johnson

This is a main-course pasta salad featuring the delicious chemistry of marinated artichoke hearts and beer-steamed Italian sausage.

Beermate: Remembering that artichokes make everything tasted after them seem sweeter and being conscious of the spice in the sausage, it makes sense that a somewhat hoppy beer would best suit this salad. Perhaps a best bitter such as Bateman XXXB or Left Hand Sawtooth Ale.

Before You Begin: Bottled or canned artichoke hearts may not be wonderful for consumption plain, but they work marvelously in pasta salads like this one.

3/4 cup brown ale
2 mild Italian pork sausages
1/2 cup chopped onion
2 cloves garlic, chopped
14-oz tin pitted black olives, sliced
1 cup marinated artichoke hearts, quartered
1/2 cup grated Romano cheese
1 tsp tarragon vinegar (or other herb vinegar)
Salt and pepper to taste
1/2 lb linguine, or any pasta of choice
1 large red pepper, julienned

In a medium-size pan on medium heat, add the ale and sausages and steam until the sausages are cooked. Remove the sausages and slice into 1/4-inch pieces. In the same pan with the sausage liquid, sauté the onion and garlic until the onion is translucent.

Combine the olives, artichoke hearts, cheese, vinegar and salt and pepper in a large bowl and add the sausage, onion and garlic. Mix well and set aside for the flavors to blend.

Cook the pasta in salted water until al dente. Drain and combine with the sausage mixture. Toss well and serve garnished with red pepper slices.

Serves 8.

Rotisserie Chicken Salad

From: Portland Brewing Company, Brewhouse, Taproom and Grill
Portland, Oregon, USA

Created by Chef Tony Heyman and Pastry Chef Armin O'Brien

This dish is by anyone's definition a meal on its own.

Beermate: Keep the beer partner simple. Try a traditional weizen like the Portland Bavarian Style Weizen or an American wheat ale such as the Anchor Wheat Beer.

Before You Begin: If you can't find a wood-roasted chicken, barbecuing your chicken on very low heat with the lid closed should give it a smoky flavor.

For the Vinaigrette:
3/4 cup plus 1 tbsp white wine vinegar
2 tbsp minced garlic
1 tbsp each kosher salt and sugar
1 tsp each ground black pepper and crushed red pepper
1 tsp each dried oregano, thyme and marjoram
1 tsp each stout and Scottish ale
1 cup vegetable oil

For the Salad:
2 cups mixed salad greens
1½ cups coarsely chopped chicken, wood-roasted and cooled
1 cup bowtie pasta, cooked and cooled
1/2 cup crumbled feta cheese
1/2 cup fresh croutons (1/4 cup if using packaged croutons)
1/4 cup shredded carrot
1/4 cup each finely chopped green and red peppers
1/2 cup kalamata olives (marinated black olives)
1/4 cup whole hazelnuts

To make the vinaigrette, combine all the ingredients except for the oil in a blender or food processor and mix thoroughly. With the blender running, slowly drizzle in the salad oil, blending until the dressing is emulsified. Store in the refrigerator while preparing the salad. (It will keep 10 days.)

Toss all of the salad ingredients together in a large salad bowl. Serve on plates and drizzle with vinaigrette.

Serves 4.

Grilled Shrimp Salad

From: Crescent City Brewhouse
New Orleans, Louisiana, USA

Created by Chefs David Weibelt, Chester Webb, Donald Blunt

Zesty and delicious, this makes for a perfect meal on a sunny afternoon.

Beermate: This demands a spicy beer for accompaniment. I'd suggest a weizenbock like Erdinger Pinkantus or Schneider Aventinus.

Before You Begin: Get the freshest shrimp possible for this salad.

For the Salad:
8 oz fresh mixed baby greens
6 slices bacon, fried and finely chopped

For the Peanut Vinaigrette:
2 cups peanuts, finely chopped
1/2 cup vegetable or peanut oil
1/2 cup sesame oil
1/2 cup plus 1 tbsp rice vinegar
1 tbsp white pepper
2 tbsp hot pepper sauce

For the Shrimp with Pesto Sauce:
1/2 cup olive oil
6 leaves fresh finely chopped basil (or 1/2 tsp dried)
2 cloves garlic minced
1 tbsp chopped pine nuts (almonds may be substituted)
1 tbsp grated Romano cheese
1/2 tsp dried thyme
1/4 tsp lemon juice
1/2 lb fresh, shelled shrimp on skewers

Prepare the salad and divide among four individual plates. Combine peanuts, oils, vinegar, white pepper and hot pepper sauce in a bowl. Whisk well until blended and set aside.

Combine the olive oil, basil, garlic, pine nuts, Romano, thyme and lemon juice and mix well to make the pesto sauce. Cook the shrimp over an open flame, basting regularly with the pesto sauce, and carefully turning the skewers to ensure even cooking. When the shrimp are firm, remove from flame and arrange them on the salad plates. Dress salads with the vinaigrette.

Serves 4.

Scallop Seviche

From: Pepperwood Bistro
Burlington, Ontario, Canada

Created by Chef Alex Mickalow

If you like scallops as I do, then this summer salad is sure to delight. The lightly citric flavor comes both from the lime juice marinade and the Belgian-style wheat beer.

Beermate: With dining on scallops, it is important to select a beer that will not overpower the delicate flavor of the mollusks. In this case, I suggest the same beer used in the recipe, a Belgian-style wheat beer, also known as white beer, such as the Hoegaarden White or Blanche de Bruges.

Before You Begin: Be very careful when cooking the scallops for this recipe, as the overnight marinade will have "cooked" them a bit already.

For the Salad:
12 large sea scallops, cut into quarters
Juice of 3 limes
2 ripe avocados, diced
3/4 cup Belgian-style wheat beer
1 head radicchio

For the Dressing:
3 tbsp diced red peppers
3 tbsp olive oil
1 tbsp minced onion
1 tbsp finely chopped parsley
Salt and pepper to taste

The day before, place the scallops in the lime juice and store in a sealed container in the refrigerator overnight.

The day of serving, mix the red peppers, olive oil, onion, parsley, and salt and pepper in a bowl and set aside. When you're ready to serve, lightly sauté scallops in half the beer until they begin to firm and change color. When the scallops are done, add them along with the avocado and the rest of the beer to the dressing mixture. Allow to cool.

Serve on a bed of radicchio.

Serves 4 as an appetizer, 2 as a main course.

Mesclun Greens with Baked Pecan-Crusted Goat Cheese and Caramelized Apple-Shallot Vinaigrette

From: Gordon Biersch Brewing Co., Inc.
San Francisco, California, USA

Created by Corporate Chef Kelly Degala

This salad features an explosion of flavors as the sweet pecans meet the tart apples and the goat cheese rounds everything out beautifully.

Beermate: For this kind of a combination of sweet and tart, I'd suggest that a non-traditional fruit lambic would be just the thing. Try a Lindemans Pecheresse or a Mort Subite Cassis.

Before You Begin: Mesclun mix is a blend of wild greens such as dandelion, arugula and lamb's lettuce which can often be found in supermarkets, or you can make your own, from any combination of greens. *Aji-mirin* is a Japanese cooking sake; if you can't find it, just use regular sake. The vinaigrette can be served either warm or cold.

For the Vinaigrette:
2 Granny Smith apples, peeled and seeded
3 shallots, peeled and finely chopped
1/4 cup aji-mirin (Japanese cooking sake)
1 tbsp peeled and finely chopped ginger
1/4 cup rice wine vinegar
2 tsp Dijon mustard
1/2 cup extra virgin olive oil
Salt and pepper to taste

For the Salad:
1/4 lb pecans
1/2 lb goat cheese
1 lb mesclun mix
1 Belgium endive, cleaned
1 head radicchio, cleaned
1 red pepper, seeded, cored and finely chopped
2 apples, julienned

First make the vinaigrette. Sauté the apples and shallots over medium heat until caramelized and the apple is tender. Deglaze the pan with the aji-mirin and reduce for 1 minute. Transfer the apples and liquid to a blender and purée. Add the ginger, rice wine vinegar and Dijon and blend until thoroughly mixed. With the blender still running, slowly add the oil in a thin stream and process until blended. Season with salt and pepper and blend to incorporate.

For the salad, roast the pecans on a cookie sheet in a 350° oven until they are golden brown. Let the pecans cool and then chop coarsely. Cut the goat cheese into 4 disks, coat with the nuts and let it sit in the refrigerator for 15 minutes.

Trim the base of the endive and the radicchio, separate the leaves and arrange on 4 plates.

Place the cheese in a pan in a 350°F oven for 2 minutes. While the cheese is baking, toss the mesclun greens with the vinaigrette and divide among the 4 plates. Place a piece of cheese on each plate and top with chopped red pepper and apple. Serve immediately.

Serves 4.

GORDON BIERSCH BREWERY RESTAURANT
33 East Fernando Street (and 4 other locations)
San Jose, California, USA 95113
Phone: 408-294-6785

To say that the Gordon Biersch Brewery Restaurant is a success story is much like saying that Donovan Bailey, also known as the World's Fastest Man, is a fairly swift human being. Since the first of what are now five brewery restaurants was founded by Dan Gordon and Dean Biersch in 1988, the progress of the Gordon Biersch chain has been marked by tremendous achievement after tremendous achievement.

From the humble beginnings of the first Gordon Biersch location in Palo Alto, California, the Gordon Biersch Brewery Restaurant has gone on to open locations in San Jose, San Francisco, Pasadena and Honolulu, and sells its beer to over 500 other locations along the way. If this alone were not enough to count as an enormous success, the company has even gone on to open a new brewery in San Jose, with an annual capacity of 50,000 barrels, for the exclusive production of bottled and kegged beer for retail sale. Not bad for a little company less than ten years old!

As impressive as its record of astounding growth and achievement is though, Gordon Biersch would not be included in the elite brewpub company found in this book were that all it was about. No, the thing that really sets Gordon Biersch apart from the rest has been the commitment its owners have shown since day one to the concept of dining with beer.

The Gordon Biersch attitude is reflected right from the start in what they call their five locations—not brewpubs, brewing companies or brew houses, but brewery restaurants. This choice reflects what Biersch and Gordon consider important in their operations. As Dean Biersch has been known to assert time and again, it is the quality of *both* beer and food that is the key to the Gordon Biersch success.

Prior to my first visit to a Gordon Biersch Brewery Restaurant, I had little information on the company other than that it was a chain operation with, at the time, three locations. Before I had even finished ordering my lunch, however, the importance of the food part of the equation had become blatantly obvious, from the menu itself. Everywhere I looked in the packed restaurant was evidence of good food and satisfied customers. Where in most brewpubs at the time, patrons just ate food while they drank beer, here people were *dining* with beer. It was, in a sense, a holistic beer experience.

By the time I had finished my lunch and my beer, I had developed a healthy respect for the vision of Dan Gordon and Dean Biersch. And while many a brewpub and brewpub chain have since adopted the same attitude toward the conjoining of the restaurant and brewery sides of the hospitality trade, Dan and Dean will always have the satisfaction of knowing that they were among the first and the most successful.

Salad of Seasonal Wild Greens, Smoked Long Island Duckling and Lindemans Pêche Lambic Vinaigrette

From: The Pike Pub and Brewery
Seattle, Washington, USA

Created by Chef Nathan Ojala

The vinaigrette, with its peach lambic and fresh peach purée, makes this salad pleasantly refreshing as well as very tasty. It's perfect for the springtime.

Beermate: This is one case where the beer used in the dish is ideal for accompanying it to the table; select a true peach lambic like the Lindemans Pêche Lambic. If you prefer a more domestic partner, opt for a fruity ale such as the peach-flavored Wynkoop Backyard Ale.

For the Salad:
2½ oz mixed greens per person
3 oz smoked duckling per person, sliced

For the Vinaigrette:
2 fresh peaches
3 cups peach lambic
3 cups water
2 tbsp sugar
2 tbsp honey
3/4 cup raspberry vinegar
4 tbsp Dijon mustard
4 tbsp fresh lemon juice
3 tbsp finely chopped fresh basil
3 cups vegetable oil
Salt and pepper to taste

Arrange the greens in individual bowls.

Blanch, peel, seed and purée the peaches. In a pot, mix the puréed peaches with the peach lambic and warm over low heat. Add the water, sugar, honey, vinegar, mustard, lemon juice and basil and stir until well blended. Slowly incorporate the vegetable oil, stirring constantly, until the vinaigrette is emulsified. Season with salt and pepper.

Dress each salad with the vinaigrette and top with the sliced duck.

Makes enough vinaigrette for 12 servings.

THE PIKE PUB AND BREWERY

1415 1st Avenue
Seattle, Washington, USA 98122
Phone: 206-622-6044

Charles Finkel and his wife, Rose Ann, are the force behind Merchant du Vin, the pioneering beer importing company based in Seattle, Washington. Back in the dull days when diversity of beer style meant having both Bud and Coors, MdV was already breaking ground by importing some of the classic beers of Belgium, Germany and England. The going was tough, but the Finkels persevered through grit, determination and the steadfast belief that beer was a noble and complex beverage.

Along the way, Charles found that by marrying his love of good beer with his appreciation of fine food, he could more easily convince the public that the Merchant du Vin brands were something quite apart from the big-name commercial beers. As such, he has been promoting the idea of beer dinners and beer and food pairing for longer than many of us have been drinking distinctive brews and in so doing, has helped set the stage for books like this one.

The problem with including Charles in this book, however, was that he was not a part of a brewpub. True, he had the Liberty Malt Supply homebrew shop and the Pike Brewing Company as well as the importing company, but with this book featuring brewpubs, there was simply no way I could envision squeezing in any Charles Finkel recipes.

So he opened a brewpub.

Okay, so he didn't open the brewpub just to make it into this book, but the timing was certainly something quite beyond the merely fortuitous. I was out in Seattle in early 1996 scouting for brewpubs and bemoaning to Charles the fact that I couldn't offer him a spot in the book. To my surprise, he then announced that work had just begun on The Pike Pub and Brewery and that he would be glad to offer recipes were I still interested. I could scarcely believe my luck and immediately accepted the offer.

Later that day, we took a tour of both the existing Pike brewery, still known then as The Pike Place Brewing Company after the market in which it resided, and the new Pike space. The contrast was stunning. The old brewery, now but a distant memory, was a tiny hole-in-the-wall with barely enough room to swing a grain sack, while the new facility was large enough that the brewer, Fal Allen, even had an office.

The tour I took of the new pub and brewery that day did not take long; there wasn't much to see aside from unfinished walls and freshly poured concrete. Even then, however, it was fully apparent that the potential of the facility was enormous, and knowing Charles and his aesthetic sensibilities, I was confident that Seattle was indeed only months away from being gifted with yet another outstanding brewpub. Time, I'm pleased to say, has now proved me right.

Grilled Chicken with Pears, Dried Cherries and Toasted Walnuts with Pear Vinaigrette

From: The Norwich Inn
Norwich, Vermont, USA

Created by Chef Terrence Webb

To me, this salad suggests the very early days of fall, when the first hint of crispness is in the air but the weather is still nice enough for patio dining.

Beermate: I checked my initial inclination towards a fruit beer when I realized that any greater fruitiness might overload the delicious balance of the salad. Better then, a sweetish, lightly fruity and spicy Belgian-style wheat beer like the Celis White or a Blanche de l'Île.

Before You Begin: Pear vinegar is preferred for this dish for obvious reasons and it is easy to make your own by infusing quality vinegar with pear. However, you can also substitute any other fruit vinegar in its place.

For the Pear Vinaigrette:
6 tbsp pear vinegar
3 tbsp lemon juice
1 tbsp Dijon mustard
1 ½ tsp salt
1/2 tsp cracked black pepper
1 ½ cups vegetable oil

For the Salad:
1/4 cup vegetable oil
2 tbsp chopped fresh parsley
1 lemon, sliced
1 clove garlic, mashed
4 chicken breasts, boned and skinned
2 ripe Anjou pears
4 tbsp brown sugar
1/4 tsp cinnamon
1/4 tsp nutmeg
1/2 tsp salt
1/2 tsp cayenne
2 tbsp butter, melted

1 cup walnuts
Lettuce and salad greens of your choice
1 red pepper, julienned
1 green pepper, julienned
1 yellow pepper, julienned
1 bunch green onions, sliced thin
1 cup dried cherries

First prepare the vinaigrette by combining all the ingredients in a sealable container. Seal and shake to blend and set aside.

Combine the oil, chopped parsley, lemon slices and garlic in a bowl and toss with the chicken breasts, rubbing the mixture well into each breast. Place the chicken, along with any leftover marinade, into a covered dish and allow to marinate in the refrigerator for at least 1 hour.

Cut the pears in half and remove the seeds. In a small bowl, combine half of the brown sugar with the cinnamon and nutmeg and mix well. In a separate container, combine the rest of the brown sugar with the salt and cayenne and mix well. Dip each pear half into the melted butter and toss in the sugar, cinnamon and nutmeg mixture. Then coat the walnuts with a bit of vegetable oil and toss in the sugar, salt and cayenne mixture. Place the walnuts on a baking sheet in a 375°F oven until lightly toasted.

In a large bowl, toss the salad greens with the julienned peppers, sliced green onions and vinaigrette. Set aside.

To grill the chicken and the pears, place the chicken breasts in the center of the grill and arrange the pear halves on the edges. Grill until the chicken is cooked through and the pears are lightly caramelized.

When the chicken and the pears are done, thinly slice each and arrange in a fan pattern on the opposite sides of a large platter. Place the salad in the middle and sprinkle with the walnuts and dried cherries. Serve immediately.

Serves 4 to 6.

CHILI

Ale-Brewed Chili

From: The Rogue Ales Public House
Newport, Oregon, USA

Created by Chef Earl Smart

This simple and delicious chili is the perfect dish to make when you have a crowd coming over for the big game or any other informal occasion.

Beermate: There isn't a lot of intense heat to this chili—unless you wish to add it yourself—so a particularly hoppy beer isn't really a necessity. Try a full-bodied and moderately hoppy brown ale like the Golden Gate Original Ale or Brooklyn Brown Ale.

Before You Begin: As with most chilies, the simmering time is the key to this recipe's great taste, so start early.

2 lb dried kidney beans
2½ lb lean hamburger
1 onion, diced
1 green pepper, diced
1½ cups brown ale
1½ cups chili pepper ale
1/3 cup sugar
6 garlic cloves, minced
1 tbsp salt
3 tbsp chili powder
1½ tbsp dry mustard
1½ cups tomato paste

Soak the beans overnight in water.

In a large pot, simmer the beans in fresh water until tender, about 1 hour. Meanwhile, in a second large pot on medium heat, add the ground beef, onion and green pepper and sauté until the beef is lightly browned. Drain the fat. In a separate bowl, combine the brown ale and chili pepper ale. Add half of the beer, the sugar, garlic, salt, chili powder and mustard to the beef. Simmer for 15 minutes.

Drain the beans, mix in the tomato paste and add it all to the chili. Simmer for 2 hours, adding the remaining beer 10 minutes before serving.

Serves a whole gang of hungry people.

THE ROGUE ALES PUBLIC HOUSE

748 S.W. Bay Boulevard
Newport, Oregon, USA
97365
Phone: 541-265-3188

My first encounter with Rogue Ales came via a condom. The occasion was the Great American Beer Festival of 1993, where the minds behind Rogue had come up with the marvelous idea of giving away packages of condoms emblazoned with the slogan "Coming soon . . . Rogue Ales." The promotional ploy worked; the packets were the talk of the Fest and I selected the condoms as my Promotional Idea of the Year in the beer column I then wrote for *The Toronto Star.*

Condoms aside, however, at the time, the mysteries of this Rogue brewery far outweighed the facts. Other than having stopped by their GABF booth to sample a few of their beers, I knew precious little about this intriguing Oregon operation. I and the rest of the craft-brewing world were to learn a lot more in the ensuing months and years.

In getting to know Rogue, there are two individuals who figure prominently: Jack Joyce and John Maier. It has been said, and will no doubt be said many times again, that Jack is the rogue behind Rogue. Inevitably attired in sweatshirt and jeans, Jack is the seemingly indefatigable force behind the brewery, the decidedly unpresidential president who can be obstinate, argumentative and the kind of guy you would like to share a beer with, all at the same time. Like Reggie Jackson, Jack Joyce is indeed the straw that stirs the drink.

Jack's alter ego is John Maier. An easygoing brewer with a very well-documented passion for hops, John always portrays the image of the relaxed artist, equally at home in his brewery or at a blues bar. Rogue's head brewer since 1989, John has taken the use of hops in ale and made it into his own unique brand of artistry, to the point that Rogue's ales are well known in beer circles for their generally outrageous hoppiness. Unlike some of his peers, however, John always somehow manages to keep his hops in balance with the malt portion of his beer and thereby produces some of the most bitter but beautifully balanced ales on the West Coast.

John plies his trade in a converted warehouse in Newport, Oregon, just down the street from the International Society of Rogues, also known as the brewery offices and retail store, and across the bay from the Rogue Ales Public House. While up until very recently Rogue still brewed at the Public House, the equipment used for brewing has since been removed and it now operates as Newport's finest bar, serving up the entire range of Rogue ales in addition to other "guest" beers.

Rather than disqualify Rogue from this cookbook on this technicality, however, I chose instead to invoke the "grandfather clause" and include several Rogue recipes. Maybe it stems from how impressed I am by a brewer who can employ hops copiously, yet sanely, or perhaps it is just the rogue in me, but I can't help having a soft spot for this brewery.

Dragon's Last Breath Chili

From: The Kingston Brewing Company
Kingston, Ontario, Canada

Created by Chef Roger Holmes

Prunes in chili might strike one as odd, but they add an enticing richness to this dish.

Beermate: The prunes are the key ingredient in selecting a beer to partner this dish, as they furnish the chili with a full and sweet roundness. A complementary beer would be a nicely rounded porter, perhaps a Samuel Smith Taddy Porter or an Anchor Porter.

2½ lb sirloin tip, cut into 1/2-inch cubes
1 lb sweet Italian sausage, casing removed
1 large onion, finely chopped
4 garlic cloves, minced
1/2 lb pitted prunes, diced
3/4 cup beef broth
2 cups British-style brown ale
1½ cups tomato sauce
4 tbsp Mexican chili powder (chipotle chili powder is best)
1 tbsp cumin
1 tbsp paprika
1 tbsp oregano
1 tsp salt

In a large pot, cook the beef and sausage until well browned and remove from the pot. Sauté the onion and garlic in the drippings until they are golden and fragrant. Stir in the prunes and broth and bring the mixture to a boil. Stir in browned meat and sausage, ale, tomato sauce, chili powder, cumin, paprika, oregano and salt. Bring the chili back to a boil and reduce the heat. Simmer covered for 2 hours or until the beef is tender.
    Serves 4 to 6.

Louisiana/Texas-Style Chili with Ale

From: The Mendocino Brewing Company
Hopland, California, USA

Created by H. Michael Laybourn

This chili uses a mélange of Texas, Cajun and Mexican styles.

Beermate: With its intense flavor, this chili demands a powerful beer. Try a strong, hoppy ale like the Eye of the Hawk Select Ale or the Wild Goose Snow Goose Ale.

Before You Begin: Try to make it at least a day ahead of time, if possible.

1 tsp vegetable oil
2 lb round steak, cubed
2 tbsp Cajun seasonings
1 tbsp butter
1/2 cup each finely chopped green pepper and celery
1 each large onion and carrot, finely chopped
3 cloves garlic, minced
1 large jalapeño pepper, seeded and finely chopped
5 tbsp each chili powder and cumin
2 tsp thyme
1 tbsp each salt and oregano
1/2 cup chopped fresh coriander
14-oz can tomatoes with juice, chopped
Two 8-oz cans tomato sauce
Hot pepper sauce (to taste)
1 tbsp chocolate chips
12 oz brown ale
2 tbsp cornmeal

In a sauté pan on medium, heat the vegetable oil and add the meat and Cajun seasonings. In another large pot, also on medium heat, sauté the green pepper, celery, onion, carrot, garlic and jalapeño in the butter. When the meat is browned, add it to the vegetables and mix well. Add the chili powder, cumin, thyme, salt, oregeno and coriander, stirring them into meat and vegetable mixture. Add the tomatoes, tomato sauce and hot pepper sauce. Bring to a boil and reduce to simmer. Add the chocolate, ale and cornmeal and cook for 35 minutes, stirring occasionally. Remove the chili from the heat and allow to cool, overnight in the refrigerator if possible. Reheat to serve with rice, hominy or black beans.
    Serves 6.

Zip City Buffalo Chili

From: Zip City Brewing Company
New York, New York, USA

Created by Zip City kitchen staff

Buffalo has become quite a popular meat of late and for good reason; it is rich in flavor and relatively lean compared to beef. This chili provides a terrific showcase for its marvelous taste.

Beermate: The combination of buffalo, beef, the two beans and the chick-peas gives this dish a full, complex and intriguing flavor. It pairs very nicely with a German-style dunkel such as the Thomas Kemper Bohemian Dunkel or a bock like Zip City's own or the Uff-da Bock of New Glarus Brewing.

Before You Begin: If buffalo is not your thing, this recipe works well with ground beef or turkey, as well. Either way, it tastes best on the second day, so try to make this ahead of time, if you can.

1/3 cup dried pinto beans
1/3 cup dried white beans
2 cups chopped onions
3 tbsp olive oil
1½ tbsp minced garlic
1¼ lb ground beef
1¼ lb ground buffalo
3 tbsp chili powder
3 tbsp cumin
1½ tbsp cocoa powder
1½ tbsp paprika
1 tbsp dried oregano
1 small jalapeño, seeded and minced
2 bay leaves, tied in cheesecloth
1½ cups tomato sauce
3/4 cup chicken stock
3 tbsp cider vinegar
1 cup chick-peas (canned)
3/4 green pepper, diced
3/4 red pepper, diced
Salt and pepper to taste

Soak the pinto and white beans in water overnight. The next day, drain the beans and cook them in fresh water until just tender.

In a large stockpot on medium heat, sauté the onions in olive oil until tender. Add the garlic and cook for 1 minute longer. Add the ground beef and buffalo and cook until the meat is no longer pink, breaking up the lumps as you stir. Add the chili powder, cumin, cocoa, paprika, oregano, jalapeño and bay leaves and cook for 1 minute. Add the tomato sauce, chicken stock and vinegar and bring the mixture to a boil. Reduce the heat, cover and simmer for 90 minutes, stirring occasionally.

Add the cooked beans, chick-peas, green and red peppers and salt and pepper. Simmer 30 minutes more, uncovered or until the peppers are tender and liquid has boiled off to desired thickness. Remove from heat, discard the bay leaves and refrigerate chili. Serve the next day.

Serves 6.

ZIP CITY BREWING COMPANY
2 West 18th Street
New York, New York, USA 10011
Phone: 212-366-6333

With the popularity of brewpubs in North America growing almost exponentially since the mid-1980s, you might well expect that a cutting-edge city like New York would have been right there with the trend, opening brewpub after brewpub all across the metropolis. Such was not at all the case, however, and for three or four years following its 1991 opening, Zip City stood as Manhattan's only successful, continually operating brewpub.

A red-faced Big Apple finally caught up with the pack in 1995, however, and Zip City's solitude drew to a close with the opening of numerous brewpubs in both Manhattan and the surrounding boroughs. But while Zip City was no longer alone, it did remain unique as the only bottom-fermenting brewpub in New York City, and one of the few on the East Coast. It is a status that reflects the foresight of Zip City's owner, Kirby Shyer.

Although I have known Kirby for a number of years through meetings at festivals and conferences, it was not until a publicity trip to New York in the fall of 1995 that I was finally able to visit Zip City. As the sun was shining that afternoon and pre-Halloween temperatures were most agreeable, my wife, Christine, and I walked to the brewpub from our midtown hotel and arrived ravenous and very, very thirsty. Neither remained a problem for long.

As Christine, Kirby and I enjoyed a wonderful lunch, my reporter's instincts took hold and I asked him why he had decided to open a lager brewpub when the industry was so utterly dominated by ale breweries. The answer, he said, was to be found in my question. Having never expected Zip City to hold onto New York brewpub exclusivity for so long, Kirby explained, he had from the start been concerned about making his brewpub different from the rest. Since ale brewing, with its shorter conditioning time, was so much more practical for a pub and restaurant, Kirby had figured that lager production was one sure way to separate himself from the rest of the pack. He was right.

Of course, lager brewing alone would never have been enough to ensure Zip City's survival in the New York restaurant jungle, and so the quality of both beer and food became a hallmark of the Zip City experience. Good reviews and the brewpub's one-time uniqueness had spread its name, but it was the consistency of Zip City that kept patrons coming back, as we did the very next night of our extended October visit.

Unfortunately, Zip City — one of the great havens of lager brewing on the US East Coast — closed its doors by the time this book had gone to press.

Black Bean Zydeco Veggie Chili

From: The Twenty Tank Brewery
San Francisco, California, USA

Created by Kelleigh Trowbridge

For all of those chili skeptics who would never believe that a low-fat, vegetarian chili could taste good, here it is!

Beermate: The amount of hot sauce called for in this recipe gives you a good indication of how spicy it is—very! An American pale ale is perfect for this kind of heat, something like a Sierra Nevada Pale Ale or a Fish Tale Pale Ale.

Before You Begin: Ancho chili powder is made from smoked poblanos and adds a marvelous fragrance and flavor to this dish. If you cannot find it, use regular chili powder and add a drop of liquid smoke when you add the other spices.

2 lb dried black beans
1 tbsp canola oil
1 cup diced green pepper
1 cup diced red pepper
1 cup finely diced yellow onion
4 tbsp minced garlic
1 bay leaf
1/2 tbsp cumin
1/2 tbsp cayenne pepper
1 tbsp ancho chili powder
1/3 cup red hot sauce, or to taste
1/2 tbsp sage
28-oz can tomatoes with juice
Salt and pepper to taste

Soak the beans overnight in water. The next day, drain them, place the beans in boiling water and cook until they are tender. Drain and set aside.

In a large pot on medium heat, add the canola oil, green and red peppers and onion. Stirring occasionally, sauté for about 5 minutes and add the garlic. Continue to sauté for 10 minutes, still stirring occasionally, before adding the bay leaf, all of the spices and the tomatoes. Mix well, breaking up the tomatoes with the back of the spoon. Add the beans and mix again. If more liquid is necessary at this point, add some brown ale, porter or water. Cook for 40 minutes.

Before serving, add salt and pepper to taste and adjust seasonings if necessary. Serves 6 to 8.

THE TWENTY TANK BREWERY
316–11th Street
San Francisco, California, USA 94103
Phone: 415-255-9455

Years ago, as I was just beginning to earn my stripes as a freelance writer and beer specialist, I was approached to go on my first reporters' junket. The "junkers" were representatives of a local wine juice importing business who were interested in taking a group of writers down to California to show them the grape harvest; the "junkees," aside from myself, were mostly junior wine writers from Ontario and Quebec. Although it seemed odd that I was invited on such a trip, I accepted and it was off to California we went.

To this date, I still refer to that trip as "the junket from hell." Traveling in a pair of rented minivans at occasionally outrageous speeds, we were transported up through the interior of California from Los Angeles to Bakersfield, Fresno, Lodi and finally San Francisco. The food served to us along the way ranged from mediocre to downright bad, and the accommodations, while clean, were hardly what one might consider even remotely luxurious. In the end, I kept going for two reasons: a) I had no choice, and b) at the end of the road, there would be San Francisco.

I had visited the City by the Bay once before and enjoyed it enormously, and at that time there was not even a craft-brewing boom to serve as an added attraction. This time around, I had plans to shed my fellow travelers and visit Anchor Brewing as well as several of the city's growing number of brewpubs. For me, it was the carrot at the end of a very long stick.

We arrived too late for me to visit Anchor that day — of course! — but I did manage to get myself untangled from the rest of the group for a little brewpub hopping, which I had scheduled in advance to culminate in a meeting with a long-distance friend at a South of Market brewpub called Twenty Tank — named after the number of vessels in the brewery. Appropriately, I got there about 20 minutes early and by the time my friend arrived, I had already fallen in love with the place.

It was not until much later that I learned that Twenty Tank was, and still is, owned by the Martin brothers, two of the pillars of the early days of the craft-brewing movement. In 1986, they had opened Berkeley's first brewpub, Triple Rock, and achieved almost instantaneous success. Two years later, they had opened another campus-oriented brewpub, Seattle's Big Time, and two years after that, they completed the brewing trilogy with the opening of Twenty Tank. With its warehouse interior, trendy location and urban funkiness, Twenty Tank was quite different from the other two brew-pubs, but its success has shown that it certainly was just what San Francisco needed.

And, I hasten to add, it was at that time exactly what I needed, as well. My moment of salvation at the end of my junket from hell.

PASTAS, PIZZAS & GRAINS

Vegetable Pasta

From: Great Lakes Brewing Company
Cleveland, Ohio, USA

Created by Chef Rob Ulmann

A vibrant and colorful vegetarian pasta that is as quick to prepare as it is delicious.

Beermate: Given the great mix of veggies and flavors in this dish, it is difficult to decide on a single factor to match. However, I have always found that Vienna lager makes an excellent accompaniment to different vegetable dishes and so will recommend it here. Try Great Lakes Elliot Ness Vienna Lager or the Brasal Special Amber.

Before You Begin: Timing is everything with this dish. You want the veggies and the pasta to be finished at exactly the same time for the best flavor. One way to do this is through careful planning; the other is to cook the pasta to perfection first and then reheat it by running it under hot water when the vegetables are done.

1 lb fresh pasta
1/2 tsp salt
1/2 cup olive oil
1 tsp minced garlic
1/2 cup cubed yellow squash
1/2 cup thinly sliced portobello mushrooms
1/2 cup quartered and sliced Roma tomatoes
1/2 cup finely chopped spinach
1/2 cup navy beans, cooked
1/2 cup broccoli florets, blanched
1/4 cup unsalted butter
1/2 cup grated Parmesan cheese
1 tbsp fresh basil, sliced lengthwise into threads
Fresh ground black pepper to taste

In a large pot on high heat, cook the pasta in boiling, salted water.

In a large saucepan on medium, heat the olive oil and add the garlic, squash and mushrooms. When the vegetables are tender, add the tomatoes and spinach. Cook for 1 minute and add the beans, broccoli and butter. Cook until the butter is melted and mixed with the vegetables.

Add the cooked pasta to the vegetables and toss to mix. Transfer to a large bowl, top with cheese, basil and pepper and serve.

Serves 4.

Seafood Linguine

From: Crescent City Brewhouse
New Orleans, Louisiana, USA

Created by chefs David Weibelt, Chester Webb, Donald Blunt

It should come as no surprise that they have more than a few seafood specialties at The Crescent City Brewhouse, but this is still one of their house favorites. After one taste, it's easy to see why.

Beermate: Normally, when I see this much cream in a recipe, I instinctively select a pilsner to provide a refreshing contrast to the dish's richness. In this case, however, the seafood flavors proved to be too stong for a blond beer so I turned instead to a full-flavored dunkel, such as the Ayinger Altbairisch Dunkel or the Garten Bräu Dark.

1 lb linguine
1 extra large yellow onion, finely chopped
4 tbsp minced garlic
2 tbsp butter
1/2 lb fresh mussels, scrubbed and debearded
1/2 lb clams
1/2 cup white wine
1/2 lb shrimp, peeled and deveined
1/2 lb crawfish tails
1 tbsp dried basil
1 tbsp dried oregano
2 cups heavy whipping cream
1/4 -1/3 cup grated Romano cheese

In a large pot over high heat, cook the linguine in boiling water with a splash of olive oil until al dente.

In a large, heavy-bottomed pot, sauté the onion and half of the garlic in the butter until the onion is soft. Add the mussels, clams and white wine and steam until the clams and mussels open. Remove clams and mussels.

Add the remaining garlic, the shrimp, crawfish, basil and oregano, and sauté until the shrimp are firm. Return mussels and clams to pot and sauté together for 2 minutes. Mix in the whipping cream and let reduce for 10 minutes. Add the grated cheese to the mixture and serve over the linguine.

Serves 4.

Great Pumpkin Ravioli

From: Boston Beer Works
Boston, Massachusetts, USA

Created by Chef Robert Willis

A lovely autumn dish that makes excellent use of seasonal ingredients.

Beermate: This dish seems to cry out for a spicy beer to accompany all of the full and rich flavors in it, but I fear that a pumpkin spice beer might just be overkill. Better, then, a Belgian-style abbey ale with a nice spiciness and a little hop to handle the sherry and cream, perhaps a Chimay White or a Celis Pale Ale.

Before You Begin: Unless you have a specialty pasta maker in your neighborhood, you may encounter difficulty finding pumpkin ravioli. If this is the case, ravioli filled with any type of squash, or indeed almost any vegetable, will substitute nicely.

1 cup heavy cream
6 tbsp sherry
Salt and white pepper to taste
1 acorn squash
Pumpkin pie spice to taste
1/2 red pepper
2 tbsp pumpkin seeds
20 ravioli
1 tbsp finely chopped fresh basil

In a saucepan on medium heat, combine the cream and sherry and reduce by half. Season the sauce with salt and white pepper.

Cut the squash in half, scoop out the seeds and cut into 2-inch wedges. Place the wedges in a baking dish, sprinkle with pumpkin pie spice and bake in a 350°F oven until tender, about 25 to 30 minutes.

Place the whole red pepper in the oven on the top rack and broil for about 10 minutes or until the skin is thoroughly charred, turning occasionally. Remove the pepper from the oven and let cool in a brown paper bag. When cool enough to handle, peel and seed the pepper and julienne half of it, saving the rest for later use. Toss the pumpkin seeds lightly with vegetable oil, spread on a small cookie sheet and toast in the oven for 8 to 10 minutes, being careful not to let them burn.

Cook the ravioli in boiling water until tender. Drain and divide between 2 plates. Top each with the sherry cream sauce, 3 slices of squash, 3 or 4 pieces of red pepper, and a sprinkling of basil and pumpkin seeds.

Serves 2.

BOSTON BEER WORKS

61 Brookline Avenue
Boston, Massachusetts, USA 02215
Phone: 617-536-2337

I distinctly remember my childhood experience of going to the fabled home of the Boston Red Sox — Fenway Park. Although I was just a lad, my sense of baseball history was well enough developed that when my father took my mother and me to the grand old stadium, I knew that something special was afoot. We sat on the first-base line, about where the characters Ray Kinsella and Terrence Mann sat in *Field of Dreams*, and although I forget who played and what the final outcome was, I remember the field, I remember the hot-dogs and I remember that fabled wall in left field, the Green Monster.

That memory was foremost in my mind when I returned to Fenway in the spring of 1996 with a couple of friends to watch the Sox take on the Oakland A's. This time, however, our seats were well up in right field, there was a beam obstructing our vision and we had the most obnoxious family in North America planted in the seats in front of us. And the Sox had blown the A's out of the park by the end of the fifth inning.

We left early.

All was not a total loss, however, because refuge awaited just steps away at The Boston Beer Works. Thank the Slesar brothers for small mercies. The Slesars in question are Steve and Joe, two transplanted Ontarians who opened the Beer Works in 1992 and immediately found themselves with a hit on their hands. Housed in a former Goodyear tire warehouse, the Beer Works is one of Boston's most successful brewpubs, especially before and after Red Sox games. It is also one of the most eclectic. My friend Joan got an immediate taste of this latter quality when she ordered a Blueberry Ale and found that it came complete with fresh blueberries bouncing around in the beer's carbonation.

That eclecticism extends to the unusual ambience of the Beer Works, which can be best described as warehouse meets sports bar meets brewery meets bistro. Even the staff are eclectic, and seem to delight in raising a smile with a well-timed joke. It becomes most apparent, however, when you cast your eyes over the beer list written in chalk above the bar and find more than a dozen house-brewed beers of outrageously divergent styles. From the aforementioned Blueberry Ale to their well-lauded Hercules Strong Ale and their Flagship Boston Red, brewer Steve Slesar prides himself on the variety of his brews, which assures me that the Beer Works is capable of offering something to suit everyone.

Black Bean Ravioli in Thai Coconut Sauce

From: The Portland Brewing Company, Brewhouse, Taproom and Grill
Portland, Oregon, USA

Created by Chef Tony Heyman and Pastry Chef Armin O'Brien

This divinely decadent dish is made luxurious by the Thai Coconut Sauce.

Beermate: As rich and creamy as this dish is, its delicacy is such that a hoppy pilsner would simply overpower the taste. Instead, I recommend the parallel delicacy of a kölsch, such as the Goose Island Kölsch or Gaffel Kölsch.

Before You Begin: If you can't find fresh black bean ravioli, substitute another spicy version.

For the Thai Coconut Sauce:
2 tbsp each butter and red curry paste
1 cup coconut milk
3½ cups whipping cream

For the Ravioli:
1 lb black bean ravioli
1 tbsp butter or vegetable oil
7 carrots, shredded
1/2 lb shiitake mushrooms, or more to taste
1 lb medium shrimp, shelled and deveined
1 cup shredded coconut, toasted under the broiler for 30 seconds

To make the sauce, first heat the butter in a large, heavy skillet over medium heat. When melted, add the curry paste and let "bloom" until fragrant, about 1 minute. Add the coconut milk and reduce by half. Add the cream and reduce by half. Keep warm for serving or refrigerate until needed, up to 5 days.

If you have made the sauce well in advance, warm it in a large saucepan on the back of the stove. In a separate saucepan, bring water to a boil, add a pinch or two of salt and cook the fresh ravioli until tender. (Fresh ravioli will take only about 4 minutes to cook, dried will take about 9 to 12 minutes.)

While the ravioli is cooking, heat a large skillet over medium-high heat and add the butter or oil. Add the carrots and mushrooms to the skillet and sauté for about 45 seconds. Add the shrimp and sauté for a further 30 seconds. When the shrimp are pink, add the Thai Coconut Sauce to the skillet and mix well. Drain the cooked ravioli and add it to the shrimp and sauce and mix thoroughly.

Serve immediately; top with toasted coconut.

Serves 4.

Vegetable Lasagna with Sun-dried Tomato Marinara

From: The Vermont Pub & Brewery
Burlington, Vermont, USA

Created by Chef Tom Dubie

I have always thought that my mother made the best lasagna ever — until I tasted this one!

Beermate: The tomato component of this incredible lasagna might incline you toward a Vienna lager, as it did me, but a more potent and imposing brew is actually the appropriate choice to match the intensity of the sun-dried tomatoes. Try the Aass Bock or the stronger Brasal Bock.

Before You Begin: The Sun-dried Tomato Marinara is an exceptional sauce for any type of pasta, so you might want to double the recipe and freeze some for a later date.

For the Sun-dried Tomato Marinara Sauce:
1/2 cup olive oil
1 medium onion, diced
1 medium green pepper, diced
2 tbsp chopped garlic
2 cups tomato sauce
2 cups chopped tomatoes
1 tbsp salt
1 tbsp black pepper
1 tbsp chopped fresh basil
1 tbsp chopped fresh parsley
2 cups sun-dried tomatoes

For the Lasagna:
4 cups zucchini and summer squash slices
2 cups sliced mushrooms
1 cup red onion slices
2 cups spinach, steamed and strained
2 cups shredded mozzarella cheese
1 cup crumbled feta cheese
1 cup grated Parmesan cheese
12–15 lasagna noodles

To make the Sun-dried Tomato Marinara Sauce, sauté the onion and green pepper in olive oil in a large saucepan over medium-high heat. When the vegetables are tender, add the garlic and cook for 2 minutes. Add the tomato sauce, tomatoes and remaining spices and reduce heat to medium. Simmer for 1 hour.

If you use sun-dried tomatoes that are not packed in olive oil, in a separate pan, bring 2 cups of water to a boil and add the sun-dried tomatoes. Turn off the element and allow the tomatoes to sit for 1 hour.

When the sauce has finished simmering, drain the sun-dried tomatoes, chop and add them to the sauce. Stir thoroughly. Reserve about 1 cup of the sauce for the top of the lasagna.

To make the lasagna, cook the noodles until just tender, rinse immediately and let sit in a bowl of cool water until it is time to assemble the lasagna. In a large bowl mix together the zucchini, summer squash, mushrooms, onion and spinach. In another bowl, mix together the mozzarella, feta and Parmesan cheeses and set aside about a cup of the cheese mixture for the top of the dish.

Place a thin layer of the sauce on the bottom of a 9- x 13-inch pan, using just enough to cover the bottom. Top the sauce with 3 or 4 slightly overlapping noodles, being careful to first wipe off with your fingers as much water as possible from each noodle. Add a thin layer of vegetables, then a thin layer of cheese, then more sauce and finally more noodles. Repeat the layering process until the pan is full or you are out of filling, preferably both.

Top the lasagna with the reserved sauce and cheese. Cover with aluminum foil and place in a 350°F oven. Cook for 20 to 30 minutes, uncover and cook for a further 5 to 10 minutes or until golden brown. Let stand for 15 to 20 minutes before serving.

Serves 6.

THE VERMONT PUB & BREWERY

144 College Street
Burlington, Vermont, USA 05401
Phone: 802-865-0500

Growing up in Montreal in the dark days of pre-cable television, I remember quite distinctly the identification call of the one border television station we could pick up with our rabbit ears and, later, roof antenna. "You are watching WUTV," it cried, "Plattsburg, North Pole, Burlington."

Plattsburg might as well have been on the moon for all I knew about it and the North Pole, I was pretty sure, was the place where Santa Claus was supposed to hang out. Burlington, on the other hand, I knew. It was this city about an hour or so south, where Montrealers would go to shop for cheap clothes and from where, I would later learn, American students would come north in search of Canadian beer. One of those students was Greg Noonan.

Greg admitted this to me many years later as we discussed his brewpub, the Vermont Pub and Brewery, located in that self-same city of Burlington. It formed an odd bond of sorts between us, as we discussed the old days when most beer tasted more or less the same, and Quebec boasted the most distinctive commercial brands on the continent. We had both consumed our fair shares of Québécois ale in those days, but he had driven an hour or more to get his, while I had taken my Export, Labatt 50 and Brador pretty much for granted.

There was no risk that I was going to take Greg's brews for granted, though. Sitting there in the Vermont Pub enjoying the last bites of lunch and sipping on a wonderful Bombay Grab India Pale Ale, it was easy to understand why Greg has enjoyed considerable success in the state's largest city. Great beer, fine food and a comfortable ambience is a theme that has been repeated time and again through the course of this book, but it is one that is certainly more than applicable to the Vermont Pub and Brewery.

The president of the Canadian Amateur Brewers Association had prepared me for my first trip to Greg's brewpub by telling me to go there twice, once during the day to make tasting notes and again at night to enjoy myself. I was staying 30 miles out of town and so couldn't make the second stop, but it was easy to see why my friend had made his suggestion. Until I get back to Vermont for a night spent in Burlington proper, and the Vermont Pub in particular, I do not think that I will be able to say that I have truly experienced the Vermont Pub and Brewery.

And maybe the next time I go, I will bring Greg some Montreal beer for old time's sake. Except that I think the brand names might more likely be Unibroue, McAuslan and Brasseurs du Nord instead of Molson and Labatt.

Chicken Fettuccine in Blue Heron
Tarragon Cream Sauce

From: The Mendocino Brewing Company
Hopland, California, USA

Created by the pub kitchen staff

Fettuccine and chicken in a great cream sauce are given a little extra boost by the addition of tarragon and some fine pale ale.

Beermate: A crisp, slightly herbal pilsner will provide a wonderful contrast to the creaminess of this dish and a complement to the tarragon. Try a Whistler Lager or a Stoudt's Pilsner.

Before You Begin: This is a tasty and filling pasta dish that can be easily made with "on-hand" ingredients. Don't be afraid to substitute, but do keep the tarragon in the recipe — it adds a wonderful flavor to the sauce.

1 lb fettuccine noodles
1 tbsp olive oil
1/2 lb butter
1/4 cup all-purpose flour
1/3 cup chopped fresh parsley
5 or 6 green onions, chopped
1 tbsp chicken broth
1 tbsp dried tarragon
1/2 tbsp white pepper
1 tbsp chopped garlic
1 qt heavy cream
1 lb boneless chicken breasts, cooked and chopped
1/4 cup pale ale

In a large pot over high heat, boil water with olive oil and add the fettuccine. Cook until al dente.

In a separate pot, melt the butter over medium heat and add the flour, incorporating it fully to form a roux. Add the parsley, onions, broth, tarragon, pepper, garlic and cream and stir well. Let simmer for 5 to 10 minutes so that the flavors can blend, stirring occasionally. Add the chicken and pale ale and simmer until heated through.

Drain the fettuccine and toss with sauce.

Serves 4.

Herb-Roasted Chicken with Penne Rigate

From: Gordon Biersch Brewing Company, Inc.
Palo Alto, California, USA

Created by Corporate Chef Kelly Degala

This simple-to-prepare dish highlights the freshness of its ingredients.

Beermate: This is a classic dish for pairing with a Vienna lager such as Belle Gueulle or the Thomas Kemper Amber Lager.

Before You Begin: Dried herbs just don't cut it in this dish, so make sure that you can get your hands on fresh basil, rosemary and thyme before you start out.

For the Marinade:
1 cup virgin olive oil
2 tbsp finely chopped garlic
1 tbsp each finely chopped thyme and rosemary

For the Penne:
1 chicken, fryer-type, deboned and split
1/2 lb penne
4 tomatoes, peeled, seeded and chopped
1 tbsp each minced garlic, balsamic vinegar and chopped basil
1/2 tsp each finely chopped rosemary and thyme
2 tbsp extra virgin olive oil
Salt and pepper to taste

The night before, combine all of the marinade ingredients in a container with a tight-fitting lid and add the chicken. Refrigerate overnight.

Heat an ovenproof pan on high until slightly smoking. Place the chicken skin-side down in the pan and cook until the skin is browned. Flip the chicken and place the pan in a 450°F oven for 10 to 12 minutes.

Meanwhile, boil the penne in salted water until al dente. Drain and return to the pot to keep warm.

When the chicken is done, remove it from the pan to a plate and return the pan to the stove top on medium heat. Add the tomatoes and garlic and sauté for 1 to 2 minutes. Deglaze the pan with the balsamic vinegar and reduce slightly.

Turn off the heat, add the basil, rosemary, thyme, olive oil and cooked pasta, and season with salt and pepper as desired. Place the pasta in a large platter, top with the chicken and cover with the sauce. Serve immediately.

Serves 2.

Veggie Pesto Pizza

From: Boston Beer Works
Boston, Massachusetts, USA

Created by Chef Robert Willis

A great garlicky pizza that looks as good as it tastes.

Beermate: The strong flavors of pesto always present a beverage matching problem and that difficulty is compounded when the sweetness of sun-dried tomatoes and yellow peppers and the briny earthiness of kalamata olives are added to the mix. In the face of such a mélange of taste, I recommend the contrasting crispness of a good German-style pilsner like Hopps Bräu or the Spaten Pils.

Before You Begin: If you do not wish to use a prepared pesto, you can make your own by blending together 1 cup of chopped fresh basil leaves, 3 cloves of garlic, 1/4 to 1/3 cup extra virgin olive oil, 1/4 cup freshly grated Parmesan cheese and salt and pepper to taste. And if you wish to make your own pizza dough, I suggest using the Red Tail Pizza Crust from the Breads section (page 162).

1 pizza dough
1/2 cup pesto
Olive oil as needed
6 marinated artichoke hearts, quartered
8 kalamata olives, pitted and halved
6 sun-dried tomatoes, julienned
1/2 yellow pepper, julienned
1/4 cup grated Parmesan cheese

Roll out the pizza dough on a greased pan. Dilute the pesto with extra olive oil if necessary until it becomes a spreadable sauce. Spread the pesto thinly across the the pizza dough. Top with the artichoke hearts, olives, sun-dried tomatoes and yellow pepper strips, distributing them all evenly over the dough. Bake in a 400°F oven for 12 to 15 minutes or until the crust is a golden brown. (If using a thick crust, reduce the oven temperature to 350°F and extend the cooking time as needed, to avoid a burned crust.)

When the pizza is done, remove from the oven and immediately sprinkle with the grated cheese.

Serves 2 to 4.

316 Pizza

From: The Twenty Tank Brewery
San Francisco, California, USA

Created by Chef Kelleigh Trowbridge

The classic tomato and cheese pizza gets a boost in this version with the addition of cheddar and coriander.

Beermate: This is a classic case for combining the taste of tomato with the malty start and dry finish of a Vienna lager. Try a Great Lakes Elliot Ness Lager or a Negra Modelo.

Before You Begin: Use a ready-made pizza dough, your own recipe or the Red Tail Pizza Crust from the Breads section (page 162).

1 tbsp olive oil
1 large clove garlic, minced
1½ cups canned tomatoes, drained and diced
1½ tbsp tomato paste
1 tsp dried oregano
1 tsp dried basil
pinch brown sugar
salt and pepper to taste
1 pizza dough
1/2 lb boneless chicken breast
2/3 cup grated Monterey Jack cheese
2/3 cup grated old cheddar cheese
1 sweet red pepper, roasted and julienned
1 bunch chopped fresh coriander

In a small saucepan on medium heat, add the olive oil and garlic and sauté for 1 minute. Add the tomatoes and tomato paste and mix well. Add the oregano, basil, brown sugar, salt and pepper. Mix well and allow to simmer for 10 to 15 minutes.

Meanwhile, broil the chicken breast until done, let cool and dice. Combine cheeses, mixing well.

Roll out the pizza dough on a greased pan and cover with tomato sauce. Top with chicken, red pepper, coriander and the cheese mixture. Cook in a 400°F oven for 15 minutes or until done. (If using a thick crust, reduce the oven temperature to 350°F and extend the cooking time as needed, to avoid a burned crust.)

Serves 2 to 4.

Brew Company Barley Pilaf

From: Marin Brewing Company
Larkspur, California, USA

Created by Chef Matt Fluke

This easy-to-make side dish is almost risotto-like in its flavor and creaminess. Serve it alongside any meat or chicken dish at dinner or with mixed grilled vegetables for a nice light meal.

Beermate: The earthy flavor of the mushrooms combining with the light, tender taste of the pearl barley makes a British-style mild ale a particularly appropriate accompaniment. Try a Shaftebury Cream Ale or Grant's Celtic Ale.

Before You Begin: If you are a fan of mushrooms, using wild ones such as porcini or portobellos will make this particularly delicious.

1 tbsp butter
1/2 cup diced white onion
2 cups pearl barley
4 cups chicken stock
1 cup mushrooms
Salt, pepper and chopped fresh parsley to taste

Melt the butter over high heat in a heavy, ovenproof saucepan. Add the onion and sauté until translucent but not browned. Add the barley and mix until all of the pearls are coated with butter. Add the chicken stock and bring to a boil.

Remove the pan from heat and cover tightly. Place in a 350°F oven for 45 minutes. Adjust seasonings with salt, pepper and parsley and serve.

Serves 8 to 12 as a side dish.

SEAFOODS

Rogue Ale Fish & Chips

From: The Rogue Public House
Newport, Oregon, USA

Created by Chef Earl Smart

These fish and chips bring back fond memories of a second-story pub I used to frequent.

Beermate: Fish and chips is perhaps the quintessential pub dish and so it deserves the quintessential pub ale: best bitter. Try the Younger's Special Bitter from Rogue or the Rockies Amber Ale.

Before You Begin: Garden seasoning is a blend of dehydrated vegetables.

For the Fish:
1¾ cups all-purpose flour
2 tbsp garden seasoning
1 tbsp chopped fresh dill
1 egg
1/3 cup brown ale
1½ cups cold water
2 tbsp olive oil
8 red snapper fillets (about 2 oz each)

For the Fries:
4 to 6 large potatoes, cut into fries
3½ cups brown ale
Vegetable oil for deep frying

In a large pot, bring to a boil the 3½ cups of ale. Proceeding in small batches, blanch the fries in the beer for 3 to 4 minutes and set aside.

In a large bowl, combine the flour, garden seasoning and dill. Form a well in the center of the mixture. In a separate bowl, lightly beat the egg and add the water, ale and olive oil. Mix well. Pour the liquid into the well in the dry mixture and combine the two by gradually pulling the flour into the center. Mix until a thick batter is formed.

Heat the oil in a deep fryer, wok or heavy pot until very hot. Working in batches, fry the potatoes until done and place them in a warm oven. Dredge each fillet in the batter until thoroughly coated and fry in oil until golden brown. Serve two pieces of fish and a good portion of fries to each person.

Serves 4.

Braised Halibut with Vegetables and Herbs

From: Pyramid Alehouse & Thomas Kemper Brewery
Seattle, Washington, USA

Created by Chef Leslie Dillon

The light braising of this recipe produces fish fillets that are truly moist, flavorful and almost creamy in texture.

Beermate: The key to this dish is not letting any flavors overpower the delicate taste of the fish, and that includes the accompanying beer. Try a light hefeweizen like the Thomas Kemper Hefeweizen or the filtered Victoria Weizen.

Before You Begin: This dish doesn't take very long to cook, so make sure that you have everything for your meal ready before you put on the halibut steaks. If you want to serve with a flourish, Chef Dillon recommends piling garlic mashed potatoes in a shallow bowl, arranging the steaks on top and pouring the broth over it all.

3 tbsp peeled and finely chopped celery
3 tbsp peeled and finely chopped carrot
3 tbsp peeled and finely chopped red onion
1/4 tsp minced garlic
2 bay leaves
1 tsp chopped fresh thyme
1/4 tsp black pepper
3 tbsp unsalted butter
1 cup Thomas Kemper Hefeweizen
1 cup fish or chicken stock
1/4 tsp curry powder
pinch white sugar
4 halibut fillets or steaks (about 6 oz each)
2 tbsp chopped fresh Italian parsley

Put all ingredients except the halibut and the parsley into a large shallow saucepan over medium heat and bring to a boil. Let boil for 1 minute. Add the halibut steaks, cover and turn the heat to low. Simmer for about 8 minutes or until halibut is cooked through and feels firm to the touch when pressed.

Remove the fish to a serving platter or plates and pour the remaining broth over the halibut portions. Garnish with the parsley.

Serves 4.

PYRAMID ALEHOUSE & THOMAS KEMPER BREWERY
91 S. Royal Brougham Way
Seattle, Washington, USA 98134
Phone: 206-682-8322

For me, ballparks are very special places. Big or small, Little League or pro, there is something about a baseball diamond that never fails to move me. Even just being in the vicinity of a major-league park, even one as monstrous and un-baseball-like as the Seattle Kingdome, is enough to stir my blood and set my imagination afire.

And so it was on the day following the official opening of the major-league baseball season, I found myself less than a block away from the above-scolded oversize concrete pillbox that serves as home to the Seattle Mariners. The place was the Pyramid Alehouse, within spitting distance from the ballpark, and my host for the occasion was beer writer, Pyramid communications director and baseball indifferent, Ben Myers.

Now, given that the baseball season had just begun and that the ballpark's shadow was so very close, I would have been quite happy to sit in the brewpub for hours on end, talking about the state of the game and how the season was likely to finish up. But, as noted, Ben couldn't have cared less about baseball and besides, I was there on beer business, so beer was to be the topic of the day and baseball be damned.

What I learned over lunch that day was that Pyramid, or Hart Brewing as they were then known, was a relative newcomer to the Seattle beer scene. Not that the company was a John-Barleycorn-come-lately, mind you, but that its origins were to be found in a different town, well, two different towns, to be precise.

The Pyramid Brewing Company is an amalgamation of two early craft breweries: Hart Brewing of Kalama, Washington, and Thomas Kemper Brewery of Poulsbo, Washington. The union came in 1992 when Hart purchased Thomas Kemper and bought themselves a more complete coverage of the craft-beer market with the Kemper lagers joining the Pyramid line of ales. It was a pairing that seemed to work and Hart grew enough to eventually move northward to Seattle in 1995, opening the brewery and pub in which I sat, pondering ales and lagers and balls and strikes.

The brewpub itself is a wonderfully modern and attractive piece of design work. With its long, horseshoe-shaped bar and open kitchen, it exudes a sense of intimacy despite its wide-open spaces and high ceilings. And if the atmosphere is not enough to mellow out a person, then there are always the gentle wafts of the aroma of fresh pizzas baking in the ovens and fresh beers brewing in the kettles. Sensory deprivation this is not.

And speaking of deprivation, I never did get Ben or anyone else at Pyramid to talk baseball with me that day nor did I get a chance to take in a game during that short trip. But then again, after a wonderful lunch in Pyramid's comfortable brewpub, I didn't care.

Lake Erie Walleye

From: Great Lakes Brewing Company
Cleveland, Ohio, USA

Created by Chef Rob Ulmann

Similar to the classic Cajun method of cooking catfish, this recipe dishes up a tasty way of serving a too-often-ignored fish.

Beermate: With such a succulent fillet and rich, creamy sauce, I can think of no better accompanying beer than a pale bock such as the Stoudt's Honey Double Mai-Bock or the Ayinger Maibock.

Before You Begin: The fillets will take much less time to cook than the sauce will to make, so prepare the sauce first. Freshwater perch may also be used in this recipe.

Juice of one lemon
1/4 cup white wine
1/4 cup whipping cream
1/2 lb unsalted butter, cubed
Salt and pepper to taste
4 walleye fillets (about 7 oz each)
1 cup cornmeal
1/4 cup vegetable oil

To make the sauce, combine the lemon juice and white wine in a medium sauce-pan on high heat. Reduce to 3 tbsp and add the whipping cream. Reduce by half, turn the heat to low and slowly whisk in the butter. Season with salt and pepper; keep it warm while you cook the fish.

Dust each fillet with cornmeal. In a sauté pan on medium-high, heat the oil until very hot. Brown each filet on both sides and transfer to a baking dish. Bake in a 350°F oven until done.

Serves 4.

Northwest Salmon Poached in Apricot Ale

From: Pyramid Alehouse & Thomas Kemper Brewery
Seattle, Washington, USA

Created by Chef Rob Fritz

The unusual pairing of salmon and apricot ale lends the fish a most enjoyable, light fruitiness.

Beermate: Where this dish is concerned, the choice is yours: complement or contrast. For a complementary beer, try a light, fruity mild ale such as Shaftebury Cream Ale, or contrast the taste with a Pyramid Porter or other soft, roasty porter.

Before You Begin: If you cannot get Pyramid Apricot Ale or other apricot-flavored beer, try substituting a peach beer or a very fruity golden ale.

4 salmon fillets (7 or 8 oz each)
4½ cups apricot ale
1/2 tsp kosher salt
1/2 tsp black peppercorns, freshly cracked
3 tbsp butter
1 lemon
2 tbsp chopped fresh dill

Place the salmon in a shallow baking dish and add apricot ale to just cover the fillets. Sprinkle the top with salt and pepper, add the butter to the pan and squeeze the juice of the entire lemon over the top of the salmon.

Place in a 350°F oven for 12 to 15 minutes or until the salmon is firm. (You can test this by pressing the back of a spoon against the fillet; if there is no indentation, then the the fish is done. Alternately, you can check the internal temperature of the salmon with a food thermometer and stop cooking when it reaches 125°F.)

Remove from the oven and serve, garnishing with dill.

Serves 4.

Pumpkin Spiced Salmon

From: Boston Beer Works
Boston, Massachusetts, USA

Created by Chef Robert Willis

This glaze not only adds beautifully to the salmon fillets' existing richness, but also seals in the moisture for a mouthwateringly delectable dish.

Beermate: Choose a malty porter to set off the sweetness of the glaze and the light smokiness of the grill, while complementing the full flavor of the salmon perfectly. Try Pete's Wicked Maple Porter or Marin Brewing's Pt. Reyes Porter.

Before You Begin: With the recent proliferation of pumpkin beers, you should have no trouble finding a suitable beer for this recipe. It that is a problem, however, look for a spicy, malty brown ale or porter.

4 cups pumpkin ale
1/2 cup honey
1/4 cup brown sugar
1/4 cup pumpkin seeds, roasted and crushed
2 tbsp pumpkin pie spice
1/2 tbsp cumin
3/4 tsp cinnamon
1/2 cup orange juice
2 tbsp arrowroot
4 salmon fillets (8 to 10 oz each)

In a saucepan on medium heat, combine the ale, honey, sugar, pumpkin seeds, pumpkin pie spice, cumin and cinnamon and mix well. Reduce the liquid by half.

In a mixing bowl, combine the orange juice with the arrowroot, and use this to thicken the glaze as necessary. (Arrowroot thickens at roughly twice the rate of wheat flour.)

Place the salmon fillets on a hot grill and generously baste with the glaze. Cook for 3 to 4 minutes, reglazing as needed. Flip and repeat on the other side, glazing generously again. Serve the fillets with the remaining glaze as a sauce.

Serves 4.

Grilled Swordfish in Japanese Marinade

From: Denison's Brewing Company & Restaurants
Toronto, Ontario, Canada

Created by Chef Glenroy Anderson

This masterpiece of a marinade works as well with swordfish as it does with tuna, shark or any other firm-fleshed fish.

Beermate: Swordfish is a fish of only moderate fat content, but this marinade makes it taste luxuriously rich without sacrificing its natural delicacy. It follows, then, that the best partner for this dish would be a firm yet delicate kölsch like that of Küppers or perhaps a honey ale like the Oregon Honey Beer.

Before You Begin: Planning ahead has never been my personal forte, but I was glad I was able to think ahead enough that I let this fish marinate for a couple of days before we grilled it. Seldom has advanced preparation been so rewarding.

6 tbsp Dijon mustard
2 cups vegetable oil
1 tbsp warm water
4 tbsp soya sauce
4 tbsp rice wine vinegar
1/2 tbsp sugar
1 green onion, chopped
4 swordfish steaks (8 oz each)

In a medium mixing bowl, add the mustard and slowly whisk in half of the vegetable oil until it is fully incorporated. Continuing with the whisk, add the warm water, remaining oil, soya sauce, rice wine vinegar, sugar and green onion. Mix until evenly blended.

Pour the marinade into a lidded container, add the steaks and seal. Shake gently so that the swordfish is well coated with the marinade. Let sit for a minimum of 24 hours in the refrigerator, gently shaking from time to time to distribute the marinade. Grill, fry, broil or bake the swordfish as desired.

Serves 4.

Tortilla-Crusted Black Tip Shark with Chipotle Honey Beer Sauce

From: Portland Brewing Company, Brewhouse, Taproom and Grill
Portland, Oregon, USA

Created by Chef Tony Heyman and Pastry Chef Armin O'Brien

To my mind, shark is possibly the most underrated product of the sea, often given a backseat to such higher-profile fish as swordfish and marlin. In this marvelously crunchy-spicy recipe, though, nothing could taste better.

Beermate: The chipotles add a fair amount of heat to the sauce in this dish and the honey gives it a sweet fullness, necessitating a like-minded beer. Try a British-style pale ale like Marston Pedigree or the more American-style St. Amboise Pale Ale.

Before You Begin: Chipotles are smoked jalapeño peppers that can be found canned or dried in specialty shops. If you use dried chipotles, rehydrate them in hot water for an hour before beginning the recipe. And if you are concerned about the freshness of the tortilla chips you have on hand, Chef Heyman has good news. He reports that at the Taproom and Grill, they get even better results with this dish if they use semi-stale chips rather than fresh ones.

3 oz (1-2 snack-sized bags) yellow tortilla chips
3 oz (1-2 snack-sized bags) blue tortilla chips
1 tbsp cumin
1 tbsp chili powder
2 tsp cayenne pepper
3 egg whites
1/4 cup clarified butter
1/2 cup chopped chipotle peppers
1 tbsp honey
1 tbsp white pepper
1/2 cup honey beer
1 shallot, minced
3/4 cup heavy cream
1/2 cup butter
4 black tip shark fillets (6 to 8 oz each)

Begin by placing the tortilla chips, cumin, chili powder and cayenne in a food processor and pulse until coarsely chopped (about 45 seconds). Alternately, you can crush the chips by hand and toss them with the spices. Put the chip mixture in a large bowl and set aside.

Next, beat the egg whites in a second large bowl with the clarified butter until blended and set aside. In a food processor, purée the chipotle peppers, honey and pepper and set aside.

In a heavy saucepan over medium heat, bring the honey beer and shallot to a boil and reduce to approximately 2 tbsp of liquid. Add the cream, bring to a boil once again and reduce by half. Add the butter to the sauce in four parts, making sure that each portion is blended in before adding the next. When all the butter has been incorporated, add the chipotle purée, mix well and keep warm.

Heat a heavy skillet over high heat. Dredge the shark fillets in the egg mixture and then the tortilla mix. Fry quickly until the flesh is firm, making sure not to overcook. Serve the fillets topped with the chipotle honey beer sauce.

Serves 4.

**PORTLAND BREWING COMPANY,
BREWHOUSE, TAPROOM AND GRILL**
2730 NW 31st Avenue
Portland, Oregon, USA 97210
Phone: 503-226-7623

One of the unassailable truths about the North American craft-brewing movement is that it is an industry on the move. In as much as a decade or more or as little as a couple of years, many of the segment leaders have grown from tiny, locally oriented operations into significant regional or national players. In many cases, the changes have been almost breathtaking.

Because the typical way that a brewery grows is through an expansion of existing facilities, there are only a few places left where physical illustrations of this growth may be observed. One such place is the Portland Brewing Company in Portland, Oregon.

My first visit to Portland Brewing took place well after the brewery had expanded from its initial downtown premises to a much larger facility in a mostly industrial area closer to the edge of town. In contrast to what many might consider advisable, though, the company chose not to close down the first brewery when they opened the second, and it was there that I met with Fred Bowman, the founder of Portland Brewing Company.

The pub in which we met would be greatly complimented if I were to describe it as small; it was positively tiny! A petite sidewalk patio expanded the seating area on that sunny day, but in total there could not have been more than a dozen or so tables and the bar stretched all of six feet — if that! — across the rear corner of the room. Naturally, I had no trouble finding Fred and after introductions had been made and greetings exchanged, he took me for a tour of the brewery housed behind the bar.

Itself, the brewery was not much bigger than the pub. A rickety-looking catwalk provided increased square footage and the kegging and fermenting rooms to the side allowed greater beer production than would seem possible at first glance, but even with those additions, the tour took all of 10 to 15 minutes. It was a charming operation, to be sure, but it was also stunningly compact.

After I had seen all that there was to see, we hopped into Fred's van and took a short drive to the new brewery. I was still quite unprepared for the incredible contrast that awaited me at the end of the road and, sure enough, when we pulled up outside of the second Portland Brewing Company brewery, I could scarcely believe my eyes. I had just emerged from the prototypically small craft brewery and ahead of me now stretched a beautiful, expansive operation owned and operated by the same company!

The tour this time took closer to an hour and could easily have gone much longer had hunger not taken hold about halfway through. To sate said hunger, there was an elegant, German-style beer hall situated at the head of the brewery and a raised patio, which looked bigger than the original brewery and pub combined! Size had not adversely affected the beer, though, and the sampling I enjoyed proved to be an appetizing prelude to a plateful of what remains to this day some of the best steamed clams I have ever tasted, served, of course, with a contrasting pint of porter!

Louisiana Bouillabaisse

From: Crescent City Brewhouse
New Orleans, Louisiana, USA

Created by Chefs David Weibelt, Chester Webb, Donald Blunt

Perhaps it's not what the fishermen of Marseilles would call an authentic bouillabaisse, but it's an absolutely wonderful dish, nonetheless.

Beermate: The spice in the Brewhouse Seasonings made me think about a hoppy pilsner to accompany this dish, but all of the delicious seafood and the cup of tomatoes pointed me towards a Vienna lager. In the end, I think that the Vienna is the more appropriate, perhaps something like Abita Amber or the Algonquin Royal Amber Lager.

For the Brewhouse Seasonings:
1 tsp cayenne pepper
1 tsp freshly ground white pepper
1 tsp freshly ground black pepper
1 tsp garlic pepper
1/2 tsp paprika
3/4 tsp salt

For the Bouillabaisse:
1/3 cup clarified butter
12 oz lobster tails, removed from their shells and cut in large chunks
12 clams, scrubbed
12 mussels, scrubbed
12 large shrimp, peeled and deveined
1¼ cups Vienna lager
1/2 lb tuna fillet, sliced into 4 strips
1/2 lb salmon fillet, sliced into 4 strips
1/2 cup chopped green onions
1 cup diced onions
1 cup seeded and diced tomatoes
3¾ cups fish stock (or 2 cups clam juice, 1¾ cups water)
4 ribs Swiss chard, julienned
2 stalks salsify, cubed OR 1 cup cubed potatoes, blanched
2 tbsp fresh lemon juice
4 sprigs fresh parsley

To make Brewhouse Seasonings, combine cayenne, white, black and garlic peppers, paprika and salt in lidded jar and shake until blended. Sprinkle about 1 tbsp of the Brewhouse Seasoning evenly over all the seafood. In a large stockpot over medium heat, warm the butter and add the lobsters, clams and mussels. Sauté for about 3 minutes, stirring frequently. Add the shrimp and continue sautéing until they turn pink.

Raise the heat to medium-high and add the beer. Cook until the beer is reduced by half, about 7 minutes. Add the tuna and salmon and cook for 2 to 3 minutes longer. Discard any clams and mussels that remain unopened. Add the green onions, onions and tomatoes. Cook for 1 minute longer. Add the fish stock, reduce the heat to simmer and cook for 3 minutes. Stir in the Swiss chard, salsify and lemon juice and remove the pot from the heat. Let sit covered for 2 to 3 minutes and serve in bowls. Garnish with a sprig of parsley.

Serves 4.

CRESCENT CITY BREWHOUSE
527 Decatur Street
New Orleans, Louisiana, USA 70130
Phone: 504-522-0571

Back in 1987, I was invited to present a sociology paper at the annual conference of the Popular Culture Association. Unfortunately, I was told, there were no funds available to help defray my expenses, but they would love to hear my paper if I could make it to New Orleans.

Well, I did find a way to make it there and I did present my paper, but I must confess that I can't tell you what else went on at the conference because I didn't actually make it to any other presentations. I was far too busy falling in love with New Orleans.

As far as I was concerned, New Orleans had it all. There was a vibrant nightlife with great music clubs, and wonderful food was available pretty much anywhere and everything was cheap, cheap, cheap. In fact, the only thing that seemed to be missing from the Big Easy was good beer.

By the time I made my second visit to New Orleans for the 1990 Jazz and Heritage Festival, the beer situation had improved somewhat. Abita Brewing's beers were more easily found than they were in 1987. But even so, that was but one brewery and in most cases, but one of their brands— Abita Amber. Life for a beer aficionado in New Orleans was still not great.

By my next visit a year later though, all that had changed with the debut of the Crescent City Brewhouse. Visiting this time with my wife and a couple of friends, we had no idea that a brewpub had opened its doors within the past year. As we walked down Decatur one afternoon, it appeared to us like a vision. A brewpub! Fresh beer! We made a collective dive for the doorway.

The vision that had excited us was the product of an expatriate Austrian named Wolfram Koehler. Lured to New Orleans in 1989 on a promise of brewing opportunities, Wolf had fallen easy prey to the enchantment of the city and had decided to stay despite the failure of the brewpub deal. Scant months later, Wolf had found a location and his project was underway. The Crescent City Brewhouse opened in the early spring of 1991.

It is truly a brewpub befitting New Orleans: beautifully designed and laid out, very hospitable and with great emphasis on the excellence of the food and drink. The drink especially receives top priority, as one might imagine, and the Red Stallion Vienna lager and Black Forest Dunkel that Wolf brews are splendid examples of their respective styles. It is the Pilsner that really stands out, though, with an appetizing and quenching crispness that is found lacking in all too many examples of the style.

Best of all, no longer do beer lovers need to go thirsty in New Orleans. Which reminds me that it's time to begin making plans for next year's Jazz and Heritage Festival!

Acadian Jambalaya

From: Granite Brewery:
Halifax, Nova Scotia, Canada

Created by Chef David Shaw

This is a tremendous dish for serving at informal summer parties. Simply have every-one bring an ingredient with them and recruit volunteers to help with the cooking.

Beermate: Being a dish to serve a crowd, this naturally needs an accompanying beer that everyone is sure to enjoy. Under normal circumstances, that might be a pilsner, but the flavors of a pils would be washed away by those of the jambalaya —try a best bitter like the Redhook ESB or the Conners Best Bitter instead.

Before You Begin: This is a very user-friendly dish and has the flexibility to adapt to almost any circumstances. Chef Shaw recommends that you use whatever meat or seafood ingredients you have available.

1/2 cup vegetable oil
2 tbsp fresh lime juice
1/2 tsp cayenne pepper
2 tbsp chopped fresh coriander
2 lb boneless chicken breasts, cut into bite-sized cubes
1½ lb large shrimp, peeled and deveined
1 fresh pineapple, cored, peeled and cut into 1-inch cubes
1/4 cup vegetable oil
4 red onions, quartered and thinly sliced
6 cloves garlic, finely chopped
6 stalks celery, diced
2 medium green peppers, seeded and chopped
4 jalapeños, seeded and chopped
3 cups long-grain white rice, uncooked
3 cups chicken stock
1½ cups dark, sweet ale
14-oz can plum tomatoes, coarsely chopped (with juice)
2 tbsp finely chopped fresh oregano
4 bay leaves
1 tbsp black peppercorns, crushed
1 lb smoked ham, cut into 1/2-inch cubes
1/2 cup dark, sweet ale
juice of 1/2 lemon
2 cloves garlic, crushed

1 lb fresh mussels or clams, cleaned
2 lemons, cut into wedges
1 bunch chopped fresh coriander

Blend together the vegetable oil, lime juice, pepper and chopped coriander to make a marinade. On metal or bamboo skewers, alternate pieces of chicken, shrimp and pineapple. Place the skewers in a sealable container, add the marinade and refrigerate for at least 2 hours.

In a very large pot over medium heat, heat the oil and sauté the onions, garlic, celery, green peppers and jalapeños for 10 minutes. Stir in the rice and cook until translucent, about 5 minutes. Add the chicken stock, beer, tomatoes along with the reserved juice, oregano, bay leaves and black pepper. Bring to a boil and lower heat to medium-low. Add the ham and simmer uncovered until the rice is tender, about 20 minutes. (If more liquid is needed at this point, add more beer.)

While the stew is simmering, broil the skewers until the chicken and shrimp are cooked and lightly charred, being sure to turn them frequently so that they cook evenly. When both the skewers and the rice are cooked, remove the chicken and shrimp from skewers and add the chicken, shrimp and pineapple to the stew.

In another large pot on medium-high heat, sauté the ale, lemon juice and garlic for 1 minute. Add the mussels and steam until fully opened, discarding those that do not open. Serve the jambalaya on plates and place mussels around the edges, garnished with lemon wedges and chopped coriander.

Serves 12 to 15.

GRANITE BREWERY
1222 Barrington Street
Halifax, Nova Scotia, Canada B3J 1Y4
Phone: 902-422-4954

In the almost three years that I wrote my bi-weekly beer column in *The Toronto Star*, I had the opportunity to make numerous announcements of beer and brewery comings and goings in Ontario. Looking back, though, there was perhaps no single story that I took greater pleasure in breaking than the opening of the Granite Brewery at the corner of Eglinton Avenue and Mount Pleasant Boulevard in Toronto.

It was in my seventh column published during August of 1991 that I had the honor of running the story on the Granite and even then I had the feeling that I would be expending considerably more ink on this enterprise in the years to come. Its uptown location was good, the timing seemed to be about right and the premises, which I had viewed during construction, were large and comfortable. But what really clinched it for me were the beers: good, honest British-style ales with a lineage that wound its way through Nova Scotia and across the Atlantic all the way back to the south of England.

The Nova Scotia connection was in the brewpub's, and the brewpub owner's older brother. Kevin Keefe, elder sibling to the Toronto Granite's steward, Ron Keefe, had opened the first Granite in Halifax, Nova Scotia, as a pioneering brewpub in a long-established club called Ginger's. The year was 1984 and ever-conscious of the intense competition in the Halifax licensed trade, Kevin had decided that perhaps a brewpub would be a hard concept for his competitors to copy and one that would give Ginger's a leg up on the rest of the field. Being a man of strong will and concise action, it was not long before Kevin was busy lobbying the government to pass a law allowing brewpubs to be established in the province. And then, just as he could see the light at the end of the bureaucratic tunnel, he took a trip.

This was no ordinary vacation, mind you. The voyage that Kevin took was a journey of discovery as he spent two months in England learning everything he could about British ales and how to brew them. It involved a lot of tasting, of course, but also required his participation in one of the most intensive brewers training schools in the United Kingdom, the program of Peter Austin & Partners at the Ringwood Brewery.

All of his hard work did pay off, though, and Kevin opened the Granite Brewery at Ginger's in early 1985, making it the first modern brewpub in eastern Canada. Eventually, the Granite at Ginger's became just the Granite Brewery as the name changed when Kevin moved operations to the historic Henry House in the same city. Then of course, there was the opening of the Toronto location, and the evolution continued in 1996 with a new Granite opening in Halifax.

Brewer's Cioppino
Served Over Saffron Rice

From: The Wynkoop Brewing Company
Denver, Colorado, USA

Created by Executive Chef Big John Dickenson and
Chef de Cuisine David Allen

A seafood stew said to have been created by Italian immigrants in San Francisco, cioppino has been transplanted most deliciously here to downtown Denver.

Beermate: Try partnering your cioppino with a spicy weizenbock like Schneider Aventinus or DeGroen's Weizenbock. The spice will balance the acidity of the tomato while complementing the flavors of the anisette and fennel.

Before You Begin: It helps to think of this recipe as having three parts: The cioppino stew, the saffron rice and the seafood that goes in when the stew is being reheated. If it is available, you may wish to substitute a tomato-clam cocktail such as Clamato for the clam and tomato juices.

For the Cioppino:
1 medium onion, julienned
1 chopped bulb fresh fennel, top removed and julienned (save fennel sprigs for garnish if desired)
1 green pepper, julienned
1 tbsp minced fresh garlic
1 tbsp olive oil
1/2 cup Burgundy wine
2 bay leaves
1 tsp dried oregano
1/2 tsp dried thyme
2 tbsp anisette liqueur
28 oz canned tomatoes, drained and diced
1 cup clam juice
2 cups tomato juice
1 tsp salt
1 tsp pepper
1 tbsp coarsely chopped fresh basil

For the Saffron Rice:
1/2 cup butter
1 small onion
1/2 tsp salt to taste
1/2 tsp pepper
Pinch saffron
2 cups uncooked rice
4 cups water (substitute chicken or vegetable stock if desired)

For Serving:
Mixed shrimp, scallops, clams, whitefish or other seafood.

Sauté onion, fennel, green pepper and garlic in the oil and wine over medium heat until the onion turns translucent. Add bay leaves, oregano, thyme and anisette and cook for 10 minutes more. Add tomatoes, tomato juice and clam juice and cook for a further 10 minutes. Add salt, pepper and fresh basil; stir until mixed and remove from heat.

In a large saucepan on medium heat, melt the butter and sauté onion, salt and pepper until the onion turns translucent. Add saffron and sauté for 2 minutes more, being very careful not to burn. Turn the heat to high and add the rice and water. Bring it to a boil, reduce heat to simmer and cover. Let simmer for 25 minutes or until rice is done.

As rice simmers, add the seafood to the cioppino and reheat over medium heat. Serve the stew in bowls over the saffron rice, or bring to the table in a large bowl with the rice piled in the center.

Serves 4.

Pan-Fried Dungeness Crab Cakes with Roasted Garlic Aïoli and Märzen Beer Mustard

From: Gordon Biersch Brewing Co., Inc.
Honolulu, Hawaii, USA

Created by Corporate Chef Kelly Degala

The addition of aïoli and mustard makes for great crab cakes.

Beermate: The best beer bet is something that is malty and full-bodied. I would recommend the Gordon Biersch Märzen or Ayinger Fest-Märzen.

Before You Begin: Panko, or Japanese bread crumbs, are premium bread crumbs; if you can't find panko, use any good-quality bread crumbs.

For the Crab Cakes:
2 lb Dungeness crab (cartilage removed), shredded
1 diced red pepper
1/2 cup diced red onion
1/2 bunch green onions, sliced thin
1 tbsp Dijon mustard
1 tbsp hot pepper sauce
1½ tsp each salt and black pepper
1½ cups mayonnaise
2 tsp finely chopped garlic
1 cup panko (Japanese bread crumbs)

Crab Cake Coating:
6 cups panko (Japanese bread crumbs)
1 bunch parsley, chopped fine

Combine crab, red pepper, red onion, green onions, Dijon, hot pepper sauce, salt and black pepper in a large bowl, mixing well. Add half the mayonnaise first, mix and then gradually add the rest taking care that the mixture does not get too loose. Add bread crumbs until the mixture will hold shape.) Form into 16 crab cakes. Combine 6 cups panko and the chopped parsley to make coating. Dip crab cakes into coating until covered. Place the cakes on a pan, cover with plastic and refrigerate for 1 hour.

In a frying pan on medium-high heat, coated with vegetable oil, cook the crab cakes for about 30 seconds or until golden brown, working in batches. Flip and repeat for the other side. Transfer the cakes to a cookie sheet and place in a 450°F oven for 2 minutes, flip and bake another 2 minutes. Remove and serve immediately with the Roasted Garlic Aïoli and Märzen Mustard.

Makes 4 servings of 4 crab cakes.

For Roasted Garlic Aïoli:
3 egg yolks
Juice from 1 lemon
1 tbsp Dijon mustard
6 tbsp roasted garlic*
1 tsp kosher salt
1/2 tsp ground white pepper
3 grilled green onions, finely chopped
1½ cups vegetable oil

Place the egg yolks in a food processor fitted with a stainless steel blade and purée for about 1 minute. Add the lemon juice, mustard, garlic, salt, pepper and green onions and continue processing for another minute. With processor running, gradually add the oil in a slow, steady stream. Adjust seasonings if necessary.

Makes 2 cups.

*For instructions on roasting garlic, see Bruschetta recipe on pages 24-25.

For Märzen Mustard:
1 tbsp olive oil
4 tbsp finely chopped shallots
4 tbsp chopped garlic
1 cup mustard seeds
1/4 cup white wine vinegar
1/2 cup märzen
1 cup whole grain mustard
Juice from 2 lemons
1/4 tsp kosher salt
1/4 tsp black pepper, freshly ground

In a heavy-bottomed pan on medium heat, sauté the shallots and garlic in the olive oil. Add the mustard seeds and continue to sauté until they become aromatic. Deglaze the pan with the white wine vinegar and remove it from the heat. Transfer the mixture to a mixing bowl.

Fold in first the märzen, then the mustard, lemon juice, salt and pepper. Taste and adjust for seasoning if necessary. Refrigerate overnight for curing.

Makes approximately 2 cups.

Maine Crab Cakes with Smoked Tomato Mayonnaise

From: The Norwich Inn
Norwich, Vermont, USA

Created by Chef Terrence Webb

When the Norwich's owner, Tim Wilson, called me with this recipe, he said that the Smoked Tomato Mayonnaise is just about his favorite food in the world. After having made and tasted it, I can understand why.

Beermate: The richness of this dish necessitates a beermate with a fair amount of body and character, and perhaps a slight smokiness to match that of the tomato mayonnaise. I would suggest an Irish ale such as the Norwich's own Whistling Pig Red Ale or the lightly peated Malarkey's Wild Irish Ale.

Before You Begin: The smoking of the tomatoes really is quite simple to do, but if you wish to avoid that step, just use baked tomatoes and add a drop or two of liquid smoke to taste when blending the mayonnaise.

Smoked Tomato Mayonnaise:
3 tomatoes
1 cup mayonnaise
1/2 cup sour cream
1/4 cup balsamic vinegar
1/4 cup tomato paste
1 shallot, minced
salt and cracked black pepper to taste

For the Crab Cakes:
3 eggs
1 tbsp Worcestershire sauce
1/2 tbsp Old Bay Seasoning or other commercial seafood spice mix
1 tbsp whole grain mustard
1/2 cup mayonnaise
2 lb Maine Backfin crab meat
5 slices white bread
Oil for deep-frying

To make the Smoked Tomato Mayonnaise, first smoke the tomatoes. This can be done in a home smoker or on a barbecue by placing a foil dish of wet wood chips underneath the grill and cooking the tomatoes on a low heat with the cover closed. Either way, the tomatoes should be smoked very slowly until they are very soft.

When they are done, peel and core the tomatoes and purée them in a blender. Mix the mayonnaise, sour cream, vinegar, tomato paste, shallot and salt and pepper together in a bowl and add the tomato purée. Mix well and serve as a condiment for the crab cakes.

To make the crab cakes, place the eggs, Worcestershire sauce, seafood spices, mustard and mayonnaise in a bowl and mix well.

Place the crab meat in a large mixing bowl and pick through and remove any shell bits. (If you are using unprocessed crab meat, simply crack the shells yourself and shred the meat.) Add the egg mixture to the crab meat and toss lightly to blend. Trim the crusts from the bread slices and pulse in a food processor until reduced to crumbs. Add just enough bread crumbs to the crab mix to allow it to hold together.

Form the mix into 8 thick patties 2 to 3 inches in diameter. When ready to eat, deep-fry the crab cakes in hot oil until golden brown and crisp on the outside.

Makes 4 servings.

THE NORWICH INN
Main Street
P.O. Box 908
Norwich, Vermont, USA 05055
Phone: 802-649-1143

The Norwich Inn is one of those places that inspire love at first sight. A beautiful old inn refurbished with a mind to its historical integrity, it offers virtually everything a traveler or vacationer might need or desire, from the charm of the sleepy New England town in which it is located, to the creature comforts of recently renovated rooms and the fine cuisine served in its casually elegant restaurant. It also, of course, offers house-brewed beer.

My wife and I discovered The Norwich Inn while on a trip through Vermont, during which we traveled the state from north to south and then east to west across the southern portion. We were expected at the Catamount Brewing Company, a craft brewery in White River Junction near the New Hampshire border. We had no plans to stay in Norwich, of which we knew only that it was located a shade north of White River Junction and was home to a brewpub. At almost the last minute, we decided to stop in Norwich for the night and were lucky enough to find that the Inn did have a vacancy.

Following a warm welcome and check in, we took to the streets — well, street — of Norwich and discovered that the town did indeed live up to its billing as a quiet academic retreat. The leaves were just beginning their transition to the glorious colors of a New England fall and the serene atmosphere we encountered during our stroll was just what we needed after a day spent on the road, stopping here, there and seemingly everywhere. Our good moods accelerated when we ventured to the long, thin and cosy bar of The Norwich Inn that evening. One look in Jasper Murdock's Alehouse, as the bar was named, convinced me that here was a spot in which I could very happily spend a few hours relaxing, and one sip of the beer was enough to put to rest any hesitations that may have lingered.

At the time, the Norwich was the smallest brewpub in North America, producing a mere 75 to 85 barrels annually and operating out of a converted kitchen in the house inhabited by the Norwich's proprietors, Sally and Tim Wilson. From this impossibly small brewery came a mixture of malt extract and full-grain ales of impressively high quality, including the finest malt extract-brewed beer I have ever tasted, the Stackpole Porter.

Since then, Tim Wilson, who brews the Norwich's beers, has built a larger, full-grain brewery on land adjacent to the Inn and increased his brewing capacity considerably. It is still no brewing monolith, but Tim says that at least now they won't be running out of beer, as they did with a fair regularity in the past.

A historic New England inn, a quiet oasis on the Vermont–New Hampshire border, delicious food, great beer brewed on the premises and even a resident ghost. I ask you, what more could any traveler desire?

Littleneck Clams Steamed with Pilsner and Apple Cider

From: The Zip City Brewing Company
New York, New York, USA

Created by the Zip City kitchen staff

The combination of pilsner, cider and ginger gives these clams a unique and intriguing taste. A truly innovative variation that has proven to be a mainstay of the Zip City menu.

Beermate: You have a choice, either the pilsner or the apple cider you use in the recipe.

12 littleneck clams
1 cup pilsner
1 cup apple cider
1 small piece ginger, peeled and minced
1 tbsp butter
1 green onion, thinly sliced

Scrub clam shells well under cold water.

Place beer and cider in a large sauté pan. Add the minced ginger and clams, cover and cook until clams open. (Discard any that do not open.) Remove the clams to a large bowl. Whisk the butter into the liquid, blend well and pour over the clams. Garnish with sliced green onion.

Serves 1.

Manila Clams Steamed in Wixa Weisse Beer, Garlic Butter and Red Peppers, and Served with Parmesan Cheese

From: The Wynkoop Brewing Company
Denver, Colorado, USA

Created by Executive Chef Big John Dickenson and
Chef de Cuisine David Allen

These clams are steamed slowly over a low heat giving them a beautifully fragrant appeal as all of the ingredients open up aromatically.

Beermate: Enjoy the same weisse you use in the recipe.

15 Manila clams
2 tbsp butter
2 tbsp minced shallots
1 clove garlic, minced
1/4 red pepper, julienned
1 tbsp coarsely chopped fresh basil
Salt and pepper to taste
1/4 cup weisse beer
1 oz Parmesan cheese, shredded
1 tbsp chopped green onion

Scrub clam shells well under cold water.

In a large heavy-bottomed pot on low heat, steam the clams in water or weisse beer. When clams are half opened (after 4 or 5 minutes), drain off the liquid and add the butter, garlic, shallots and salt and pepper. Cover the pot and shake to distribute ingredients evenly. Add fresh basil and sauté until all of the clams are fully open. (Remember to discard any that do not open.) Turn the heat off and add the weisse beer, again giving the pot a shake to distribute. Carefully sprinkle Parmesan cheese in each clam and allow it to melt. Garnish with green onion and serve immediately.

Serves 1.

MEAT

Chimichangas

From: Bushwakker Brewing Company
Regina, Saskatchewan, Canada

Created by Chef Mike Monette

I still have trouble telling my burritos from my chimichangas.

Beermate: An Anchor Liberty Ale or a Pike IPA is a delightful accompaniment to this dish.

Before You Begin: You can use either all beef or all pork for this recipe, but the best flavors are obtained with a mixture of the two.

1 lb each ground pork and ground beef
1 small onion
1/2 cup chopped jalapeño peppers
1 tbsp each cayenne pepper and crushed chilies
1 tsp onion powder
5 cloves garlic, crushed
1 tsp each freshly ground black pepper and white pepper
1/2 tsp each dried oregano, basil and thyme
2 cloves, crushed (or a pinch of ground cloves)
3 tbsp hot sauce (or to taste)
1 ½ cups pilsner
10 to 12 tortillas, about 10 inches in diameter
2 cups sour cream
2 green peppers, diced
1 onion, diced
2 cups grated mixed cheddar and mozzarella cheese

In a large sauté pan over medium heat, brown the pork and beef. Drain off the excess fat and set the meat aside. Sauté the onion in butter or vegetable oil until tender. Return the meat to medium heat and add the onion, mixing well.

Add the jalapeño, cayenne, chilies, onion powder, garlic, black and white pepper, oregano, basil, thyme and cloves to the meat mixture and stir until fully mixed. Add the hot sauce and pilsner and reduce the heat to low. Let simmer for 45 to 60 minutes or until the beer has steamed off. (If the beer appears to be simmering away too quickly, lower the heat or add a little extra pilsner.)

On each tortilla, spread sour cream on half and sprinkle with green pepper and onion. Place 3 or 4 ounces of the meat mixture on top and cover with grated cheese. Roll up the tortilla, being sure to fold in the sides as you go, and bake the finished chimichangas in a 350°F oven for 5 to 10 minutes. Serve with rice.

Makes 10 to 12 chimichangas or 5 to 6 servings.

Real Ale Stroganoff

From: The Kingston Brewing Company
Kingston, Ontario, Canada

Created by Chef Roger Holmes

A simple but delicious stroganoff that gets the best out of both wine and beer.

Beermate: This is a very meaty stroganoff with a taste that is full without being too rich. If you can get a take-out container of cask-conditioned best bitter from your local brewpub, that would be the best mate. If not, substitute a good bitter such as Goose Island Best Bitter or Tetley Bitter.

Before You Begin: Don't underestimate the importance of the egg noodles in this dish; get fresh pasta if you can, or very good-quality dried noodles.

4 tbsp oil
2 lb beef tenderloin, sliced into 1-inch strips
1/2 cup all-purpose flour
2 onions, chopped
2 lb mushrooms, quartered
1/2 cup red wine
1/2 cup best bitter
3/4 cup sour cream
Salt and pepper to taste
1/2 tsp nutmeg
4 cups broad egg noodles

In a large, deep pan or a heavy-bottomed pot, add oil and place on medium heat. Dredge the beef strips lightly in the flour and place in the pan. Cook the beef until browned and add the onions and mushrooms. Continue to cook for 5 minutes.

Deglaze the pan with the red wine and beer, scraping up as much flour as possible, and then reduce the liquid to half its original volume. Lower the heat and add the sour cream, salt, pepper and nutmeg. Mix thoroughly and let simmer until the noodles are cooked. (If at this point it seems that the sauce is not thick enough, dissolve 1 tsp of cornstarch in 1/4 cup of cold water and add it to the stroganoff.)

In a large pot, boil the egg noodles in salted water until soft. Strain the noodles and rinse under hot water. Place noodles on plates and top with stroganoff.

Serves 4.

Goose Island's Hex Nut Braised Beef Short Ribs

From: Goose Island Brewing Company
Chicago, Illinois, USA

Created by Consulting Chef Keith Korn

This dish proves that there is nothing quite like beer for making meat as tender as possible.

Beermate: The searing and braising, combined with the use of good ale, really brings out the full and finest flavors of the meat in this dish. Of course, that flavor is enhanced by the garlic, onion and tomato of the braising liquid and sauce, so those tastes must also be given consideration, but it is really the beef that should command your attention in the beer matching department. For me, that suggests a lightly sweet and full-bodied Scottish-style ale such as the Caledonia 80/— (Eighty Shilling) or an amber ale such as the Great Divide Arapahoe Amber.

8 beef short ribs
Salt and pepper
1/2 cup all-purpose flour
1/2 cup canola oil
4 large onions, diced
10 cloves garlic, 4 sliced and 6 whole
1/4 cup butter
6 cups brown ale
6 cups chicken, veal or beef stock
2 tbsp tomato paste
3 sprigs fresh thyme, tied together with string
2 fresh bay leaves

Season the short ribs generously with salt and pepper and lightly dust with flour. In a very large sauté pan, warm the canola oil over medium-high heat until it just starts to smoke. Add the short ribs, reduce the heat slightly and brown the ribs on all sides, about 3 minutes per side. (You may need to do this in batches if your pan is not large enough to accommodate all of the ribs.) After browning, place the ribs in a large, heavy-bottomed pot.

In a separate pan, sauté the onions and sliced garlic in the butter until the onions turn translucent. Add the garlic and onion to the ribs. Add the beer to the ribs and simmer uncovered over low heat until the beer is reduced by one-third. Cover the ribs with stock and add the tomato paste, whole garlic cloves, thyme and bay leaves and simmer covered for 1½ to 2 hours, or until the meat is tender. Be sure to shake the pot from time to time to keep the meat from sticking.

Transfer the cooked ribs to a warmed serving dish, and cover with a lid or foil to keep warm. Skim the excess fat from the cooking liquid, discard the herbs and pass the liquid through a sieve, pressing with a wooden spoon to get all the liquid out. Return the liquid to a saucepan and place on medium heat; reduce until a sauce consistency is achieved. Adjust seasoning and pour over short ribs.

Serves 4.

GOOSE ISLAND BREWING COMPANY
1800 North Clybourn
Chicago, Illinois, USA 60614
Phone: 312-915-0075

Back when I was a student, I remember being invited to a demolition party. The people who were throwing it lived in an apartment that was slated for extensive renovations, so the idea behind the bash was to get as much of the place trashed as possible before the crowbars and sledgehammers could come along to finish the job.

That long-forgotten party intruded on my memory banks during the fall of 1994 when I paid my first visit to the Goose Island Brewing Company in Chicago. While the connection might on the surface seem odd, it actually was quite logical: Goose Island was at the time suffering through the partial demolition of the building in which the pub was located! In fact, while we were taking a tour, Goose Island owner, John Hall, pointed out the plastic covering the wall at the very far end of the pub. Behind that sheet, he said, would soon be, well, nothing.

Fortunately for Ohio beer lovers, Goose Island not only survived the demolition, but sprang back with renewed life and vigor. Of course, I really do not think that the packed house at the Goose that night even noticed the plastic sheets, much less cared about the destruction taking place on the other side of them. Had anything happened to the wonderfully authentic Goose Island Kölsch or the nutty Hex Nut Brown Ale, they might have noticed, but to the building in which they were enjoying their pints — nah.

First opened in the spring of 1988, Goose Island has been a fixture on the edge of Chi-town's Lincoln Park's neighborhood ever since. Housed on a couple of floors in a converted factory building, the brewpub quickly drew a dedicated following and boasts one of the most widely mixed clientele seen in the North American brewpub business, from blue collar to white collar, families to singles and uptown types to downtown folk.

In 1995, the brewpub expanded in a big way with the opening of the Goose Island Brewing Company, a separate craft-brewing business catering to the retail consumer with bottles and kegs of the same beers that are served on tap in the brewpub. It was a huge move for the father and son team of John and Greg Hall who run the business, but one that has proven to be a boon to both Goose Island and the Chicago beer scene in general.

The craft-brewing market in the American Midwest was one of the slowest to develop over the early years of the modern beer renaissance, and area pioneers like the Halls and the Chicago Brewing Company had a rough go of it in the beginning. As the 1990s head into the next century, however, the craft-beer market in the Midwest, and in particular in Chicago, appears to be healthy and on the move. And as long as Goose Island is not forced to host any more "demolition parties," the future looks pretty bright.

Porter Beef Ribs

From: Bushwakker Brewing Company
Regina, Saskatchewan, Canada

Created by Chef Mike Monette

I first tried these ribs at the Bushwakker and was truly taken with their great flavor and incredible tenderness.

Beermate: The spiciness of these ribs suggests to me a robust porter accompaniment. Try Bushwakker's own Palliser Porter or the Cold Cock Winter Porter.

Before You Begin: Serve with your favorite barbecue sauce or the Bushwakker Porter Rib Glaze of 1½ cup porter, 3 cups thick barbecue sauce, 1½ tbsp liquid smoke and 2 tsp crushed chili peppers. This recipe also works well with pork ribs.

2 racks of beef ribs
2½ cups porter
1/2 cup vegetable oil
1/4 cup sesame oil
1/2 cup dry sherry
1 tbsp liquid smoke
1/2 cup honey
Juice of 1 orange
1 tbsp paprika
6 or 7 cloves garlic, crushed
1 small onion, diced
1 tsp each kosher salt, thyme, oregano and marjoram
1½ tsp black peppercorns, crushed
1 tsp crushed dry chilies OR chili flakes

Cut the racks into individual ribs and place in a very large bowl. In a separate bowl, combine all the remaining ingredients and mix well to create the marinade. Pour the marinade over the ribs and let sit in the refrigerator for at least 24 hours, rotating the ribs at least once.

Place the ribs in a large casserole dish and pour the marinade overtop. Cover and cook at 300°F for 2 to 3 hours, rotating the ribs at least once. The ribs are ready when the meat flakes easily off the bones.

Serves 2 to 4.

Blackened Pork Loin with Orange–Chipotle Relish

From: Dock Street Brewing Company
Philadelphia, Pennsylvania, USA

Created by Chefs Richard Barlow and Paul Trowbridge

Simple to make but exotic on the table, this recipe is ideal for a summer or fall dinner party.

Beermate: While the heat in this dish might prompt you to reach for a hoppy pilsner, the fruitiness of the relish is such that a lightly chilled British-style pale ale may be the better choice. Try a Pike Pale Ale or the Adnam's Broadside Ale.

Before You Begin: One of the things that make this recipe so simple is the use of good-quality, commercially prepared blackening spice mix and canned chipotles in adobo. (Chipotles are smoked jalapeños and adobo is the rich tomato sauce in which they are often packaged.) Ask your favorite market for the best available brands.

For the Relish:
1/4 cup chopped chipotle peppers, in adobo
10 oranges, peeled, segmented, seeded and coarsely chopped

For the Pork Loin:
1 pork loin (4 to 5 lb), boned, trimmed, rolled and tied
(your butcher can do this for you)
Blackening spice as needed

In a bowl, mix together the chipotles, oranges and reserved adobo. Taste and add more chipotles if desired. Refrigerate until needed.

On the stove or outside grill, heat a large roasting pan until it becomes smoking hot. Completely coat the pork loin with blackening spice while the pan is heating. Sear the pork loin in the roasting pan, turning as necessary so that the loin is blackened on all sides but not burned. Complete cooking in a 450°F oven, being very careful not to overcook or the pork will become dry. Serve with the relish and basmati rice.

Serves approximately 14.

"Peculiar" Pork Tenderloin

From: The Granite Brewery
Halifax, Nova Scotia, Canada

Created by Chef David Shaw

Named not for its strangeness, but after the Granite's own Peculiar Ale.

Beermate: The sweet spiciness of this dish makes me think of one beer only—bock. Try Granville Island Bock or the New Glarus Uff-da Bock.

Before You Begin: If you are watching your fat intake, low-fat sour cream and low-fat whipping cream may be substituted in this dish. However, if you do this, the cooking time of the sauce will have to be extended.

3/4 cup whipping cream
1/2 cup each sour cream and brown ale
1/2 tbsp Dijon mustard
1 tbsp brown sugar
1 tsp minced garlic
1 tbsp crushed whole allspice
1/2 tbsp crushed green peppercorns
1 tbsp crushed black peppercorns
4 tbsp olive oil
1 tbsp each finely chopped red onion and green onion
1 slice bacon, cooked until crisp and finely chopped
1 lb trimmed pork tenderloin, sliced in 1/4-inch medallions

In a large bowl, combine the whipping cream, sour cream, ale, mustard, brown sugar, garlic, allspice and green and black peppercorns. Mix well and set aside. (This sauce may be made a day ahead of time and stored in the refrigerator, if desired.)

In a large, heavy-bottomed pan, heat the olive oil on medium heat and add the bacon and red and green onion. Sauté until the onion has become lightly browned and add the pork. Cook the meat, stirring, until it is browned on both sides and firm in the center, about 3 to 4 minutes. Remove the pork and set aside.

Return the pan to the burner, raise the heat to medium-high and add the sauce. Cook until it is reduced by about one-quarter and has thickened enough to cling to the pork. Lower the heat to simmer and return the pork to the pan to reheat. Serve when the pork is hot.

Serves 4.

Pork Rouladen with Dusseldorf Cream Sauce

From: Stoudt's Black Angus Restaurant
Adamstown, Pennsylvania, USA

Created by Executive Chef Chris Dunn

Although this extraordinary dish looks and tastes rich, it is oddly enough fairly light on the stomach. Combined with its ease of preparation, this makes it excellent for dinner parties.

Beermate: With all this cream and cheese, you might think that a pilsner would be needed to cut the richness of this dish, but the flavors of the sauce make a Dortmunder export lager more appropriate. Try Stoudt's own Export Gold or a Dortmunder Union Export.

Before You Begin: Bockwurst is a sausage of veal or veal and pork flavored with chopped parsley and chives. If you cannot find it, substitute any good veal or pork sausage.

For the Cream Sauce:
4 cups whipping cream
2 cups Dusseldorf mustard

For the Pork Loin:
1½ lb boneless pork loin (cut into 4 equal pieces and pounded flat)
2 bunches spinach, cleaned and trimmed of stems
4 pieces of bockwurst, casing removed
2 cups shredded Swiss cheese

In a large pan on medium heat, cook the whipping cream until reduced by half. Add the mustard and blend until smooth. Keep hot while preparing the pork loin, stirring occasionally.

Lay out the flattened pork loin pieces and distribute the spinach evenly over each piece. Top the spinach with crumbled sausage and distribute the cheese evenly over all. Roll up each pork loin and tie with string.

Bake the rolled loins at 400°F for 15 minutes or until done. Serve smothered in sauce.

Serves 4.

Sesame Medallions of Pork with Honey-Mustard Glaze

From: The Marin Brewing Company
Larkspur, California, USA

Created by Matt Fluke

This versatile dish provides a change of pace from the standard barbecue fare in the summer and also cooks beautifully in the oven in the winter.

Beermate: The sesame seeds lend a nuttiness to this dish while the glaze provides a subdued sweetness, leading me to think of a light, slightly sweet and spicy brew to serve as an accompaniment. Try a Belgian-style white beer like Blanche de Chambly or Hoegaarden White for a real taste treat.

Before You Begin: The key to the flavor of this dish lies in the glaze, so don't be stingy.

1/2 cup honey
1/4 cup mustard
1/4 cup orange juice
1 tsp Worcestershire sauce
1/2 tsp onion powder
2 lb pork loin, trimmed of fat
2 tbsp sesame seeds
1 tbsp olive oil

In a large bowl, combine the honey, mustard, orange juice, Worcestershire sauce and onion powder and blend. Place in a saucepan on medium heat and bring the glaze to a boil while whisking well. Remove from heat and set aside.

Cut the pork loin into eight pieces and pound each until it is about 1 inch thick. Press sesame seeds firmly onto each side of each medallion. Heat the oil in a sauté pan until almost smoking and quickly sear both sides of medallions until brown.

Transfer the medallions to a hot grill and cook until done, basting generously with the glaze. Or alternatively, place the medallions in a pan in a 375°F oven and bake 15 to 20 minutes or until done, basting generously with the glaze. Serve while hot.

Serves 4.

Globe Brewery & Barbecue Company's Arizona-style Barbecued Ribs

From: Globe Brewery & Barbecue Company
Globe, Arizona, USA

Created by Candy Schermerhorn

Candy tells me that the cardinal rule of any barbecue establishment is that you never give away your barbecue sauce recipe. I say that rules are meant to be broken.

Beermate: These ribs are intensely flavorful and intensely delicious, deserving of an equally intense beermate. Because of their smokiness, I would suggest a smoked beer, either a traditional German-style like the Schlenkerla Rauchbier or a smoked ale like Rogue Smoke.

Before You Begin: While they make their own enchilada sauce at the Globe Brewery, there are many commercial versions available that may be used instead. As for the chipotle chilies, they are smoked jalapeños canned in a rich adobo sauce and should be available in any good Hispanic or specialty-food shop.

For the Spice Rub:
1/3 cup mild chili powder
3 tbsp freshly ground allspice
3 tbsp garlic powder
1 tbsp onion powder
1 tbsp ground black pepper
1 tbsp ground cumin
1 tbsp ground coriander

For the Ribs:
3–4 large racks of pork ribs
1/4–1/2 cup porter or rauchbier
4 cups enchilada sauce
1 cup lightly hopped porter
1⅓ cups molasses
1/3 cup honey
1/3 cup bourbon whiskey
2 tbsp finely minced chipotle chilies

In a small bowl, combine all of the spices in the dry spice rub mixture, stirring to blend. Set aside 1/3 cup of the mixture. Lightly moisten the ribs with porter or, if the ribs are to be baked and a smoky flavor is desired, rauchbier. (Alternatively, a little liquid smoke can be mixed in with the porter.) Thoroughly rub each rack with the spice mixture, cover and refrigerate for 6 to 24 hours. (Any excess spice rub may be stored in a glass jar for future use.)

Roast or smoke the ribs at a very low heat (225°F to 250°F) until the meat is very tender. While the ribs roast, prepare the barbecue sauce by combining the enchilada sauce, porter, molasses, honey, whiskey, chipotle chilies and the reserved spice mixture in a large, heavy saucepan. Bring to a low simmer and cook, stirring frequently until reduced and thickened to a rich sauce (50 to 60 minutes).

When the ribs are cooked, remove them from the heat and slather generously with the sauce. Cover with a tight-fitting lid or foil and let sit 45 to 50 minutes before serving. Do not skip this step; it will ensure that the ribs are juicy and tender and have absorbed all of the sauce flavors. Serve any remaining sauce at the table for dipping.

Serves 4 to 6.

GLOBE BREWERY & BARBECUE COMPANY
190 N. Broad Street
Globe, Arizona, USA 85501
Phone: 520-425-8227

Of all the brewpubs featured in this book, the Globe Brewery & Barbecue Company of Globe, Arizona is the one about which I know the least. In fact, as I write these words in the fall of 1996, the Globe Brewery has yet to open its doors to the public!

So how do I know that it is one of the finest brewpubs in North America when it hasn't even begun operations? The answer to that is contained in one name: Candy Schermerhorn.

I honestly forget how or when I first heard of Candy, but in the years that have passed since, we have become terrific friends. It is a friendship based on not only a commonly held passion for beer, but also a love of food and drink in general, and of life. And it is a friendship that has survived despite the fact that we have never even met in person!

Of all of the North American chefs who cook with beer, Candy has to number among the finest. Her *Great American Beer Cookbook*, while not the first such book published in North America, is without question the definitive one. In it, Candy embraces the continent-wide craft-brewing renaissance and takes it wholly into the kitchen, offering recipes of a most diverse nature that feature beers of all sorts among their ingredients. To experienced chef and beer aficionado alike, it is a treasure.

And so, when I heard that Candy intended to open a brewpub with her husband in Globe, Arizona, I knew immediately that it was destined to become one of the gastronomic treasures of the brewpub world. That was my first impression. Then when I heard from Candy exactly what she had in mind for the place and saw the photos of the beautifully ornate mahogany bar she had purchased to dominate the main floor level, I knew for sure that Globe was well on its way to becoming a beer-and-food-lover's destination.

By building her brewpub in an architecturally relevant building in a town on the historic Old West Highway, and located only 90 minutes from Phoenix, Candy has assured herself of a significant tourist trade. In truth, however, I have to believe that regardless of where she had located this monument to good taste, it would inevitably be a hit. Great food, a top-quality brewing system, a barbecue sauce that eclipses by far any I have ever tasted, a fully enclosed cigar lounge and an in-house coffee roaster are surely enough to draw both visitors and residents from miles around.

Once the Globe Brewery & Barbecue Company is up and running, perhaps I will finally be able to put a face to my long-distance friend by visiting her. The only difficulty as far as I can see it, is that I might miss the area's many historic sights because I will be unwilling to pull myself away from Candy's magnificent food and drink. Ah well, we must all make sacrifices.

Glazed Breast of Chicken

From: The Mendocino Brewing Company
Hopland, California, USA

Created by Chef Megan Glassy

This dish combines two of my favorite ways of preparing chicken — marinated and glazed — and elicits a spicy-sweet taste sensation.

Beermate: The sweetness of the honey and the flavor and spice of the hot pepper sauce and soy sauce mean that this dish needs a beermate with some fruity sweetness and a touch of the hop. I'd recommend finding that combination in a brown ale such as the Red Tail Ale or Gritstone Ale.

Before You Begin: Using fresh herbs rather than dried ones will increase the fragrance of your marinade and make for an even nicer dish, but remember to triple the quantities.

1½ cups brown ale
A pinch each oregano, tarragon, cayenne pepper and paprika
1 tsp rosemary
1 tbsp olive oil
4 tsp soy sauce
4 boneless skinless chicken breasts
1/2 cup honey
Hot pepper sauce to taste

In a large bowl, combine the beer, oregano, tarragon, cayenne, paprika, rosemary, olive oil and half the soy sauce and mix well. Add the chicken breasts, making sure that each breast is well coated with the marinade. Cover and allow to marinate overnight in the refrigerator.

Remove the breasts and place them in a deep baking dish. Drizzle approximately 1 tbsp of the marinade over each breast and sprinkle with extra rosemary and paprika if desired. Place the dish in a 350°F oven and bake for 40 minutes. While the chicken is cooking, combine in a bowl the remaining 2 tsp of soy sauce, the honey and hot pepper sauce and set aside. When the 40 minutes are up, glaze the chicken breasts with the honey mixture and return to the oven for 5 minutes or until done.

Serves 4.

Smoked Chicken Phyllo

From: Swans Hotel and Pub/Buckerfield's Brewery
Victoria, British Columbia, Canada

Created by Chef John Gallichan

This variation on the Greek favorite spanakopita adds spiced, slow-cooked chicken to spinach, feta and flaky phyllo pastry for a true fusion of taste sensations.

Beermate: When the chicken is smoked or barbecued for this recipe, the resulting mixture of textures and flavors makes finding a conventional beer match a bit of a challenge. For this reason, I would recommend a rather unconventional beer, specifically a peated-malt beer such as Raftman or Adelscott.

Before You Begin: Working with phyllo can be intimidating for some people, but if you remember to keep the pastry moist, it is actually quite simple. Use a good quality phyllo and the rest is easy.

2 boneless chicken breasts
salt and pepper
1 lb fresh spinach, washed and chopped
1/2 cup chopped sun-dried tomatoes
1/2 cup crumbled feta cheese
2 tsp lemon pepper
pinch each salt and sugar
1 tsp dried oregano
1 tsp dried mint
1 lb pkg phyllo pastry
1 cup olive oil

If the sun-dried tomatoes are not oil-packed, reconstitute them in hot water for 1 hour.

Slow cook the chicken in a smoker, on the barbecue or in the oven, seasoning it first with pepper, salt and other spices if desired. Allow the chicken to cool until it can be handled easily; chop into bite-size pieces.

In a large bowl, mix the chicken with the spinach, tomatoes, cheese, lemon pepper, salt, sugar, oregano and mint. Since the spinach will lose water as it mixes with the chicken, it will be necessary to drain the mixture before using.

Meanwhile, remove the phyllo from the package and unroll the sheets, removing 2; cover the portion not being used with a clean, damp towel to keep moist.

Place the first sheet on the table and brush the top half with olive oil. Fold the sheet from the top to the bottom (creating a rectangle) and brush again with the oil. Place second sheet on top of first and repeat this process with the second sheet so that you have a rectangle four layers thick.

Facing your rectangle of phyllo, begin at the right side and fold the bottom corner up towards the top of the pastry, filling the resulting triangle with 1/4 of the chicken mixture. Now fold that triangle over towards the left so that it becomes a mirror image of the original. Fold again so that the right side of the triangle meets the bottom of the pastry. Finally, fold the remaining flap of pastry over to cover the open side and you should have a chicken-filled triangle. Repeat until the chicken mixture is completely used. (You may wish to practice with a piece of letter-size paper first so that you get all the folds right.)

Brush the pastry with olive oil, particularly at the seams, and bake in a 350°F oven for 25 minutes or until golden brown.

Serves 4.

HOTEL • PUB • CAFE
BUCKERFIELD'S BREWERY

SWANS HOTEL AND PUB/BUCKERFIELD'S BREWERY

506 Pandora Avenue
Victoria, British Columbia, Canada V8W 1N6
Phone: 250-361-3310

To me, one of the most interesting things about modern brewpubs is the number of wildly varied forms they take. In this book alone, for example, I have included British-style brewpubs like Victoria's Spinnakers, German ones such as Stoudt's in Pennsylvania, sports-oriented brewpubs like the Boston Beer Works and even the nouveau Cajun character of the Crescent City Brewhouse. There are slick urban brewpubs, rustic rural ones and just-down-the-street neighborhood brewpubs. In short, they come in all shapes and sizes and can be located almost anywhere. They can even be found in elegant hotels like Swans in Victoria, British Columbia.

The downtown Swans Hotel, Pub and Café is the creation of Michael Williams, a onetime successful sheep farmer who took an unlikely path through dog breeding and real estate speculation to arrive at brewpub ownership. While his background may have been somewhat arcane, there is no disputing the skill and savvy he has employed to build one of the most gracious and elegant brewpubs in North America.

Although it opened in 1989, my first visit to Swans did not take place until a couple of years after that and I was not to see the full facility until 1993, when I was researching my first book, *Stephen Beaumont's Great Canadian Beer Guide*. Due to time constraints, I had scheduled but one day on Vancouver Island, where Victoria is, and during that time I was to visit three brewpubs and a brewery. I was already running late by the time I made it to Swans.

Despite my tardiness, the first thing I put on my itinerary was a fully guided tour of the brewery, pub, beer store, restaurant and the 29 suites that make up the enterprise. It was without question time well spent, even though I did spend much of that time trying to keep my jaw from dropping to the ground. Everything, and I do mean everything, was so immaculately decorated and well cared for that the overall effect was of a luxury hotel with a soul. The pub was elegant without losing its comfort, the restaurant was beautifully appointed with fresh flowers adorning each table, the brewery was large and extremely well kept and each suite was luxurious almost beyond compare.

Following the tour, I sat down to a beer tasting and late lunch with Michael and discovered that the gastronomic standards of the place were on a par with the aesthetic ones. It would have been all too easy to stay and relax after my already harried day, but I was expected back on the mainland that night and still had one stop to make on the Island. To make matters even more difficult, Michael offered me a room for the evening in the hotel, which my schedule forced me to politely decline. It was an extremely difficult decision.

I have returned to Swans several times since that day and each time have enjoyed myself thoroughly. Now, however, I make sure that I never go there with a rigid travel itinerary.

Chicken Taco Pie

From: The Vermont Pub and Brewery
Burlington, Vermont, USA

Created by Chef Tom Dubie

This could just as easily be called nacho pie: the layering produces a nacho effect.

Beermate: This is not a particularly spicy dish, so try a good Oktoberfest märzen like Sprecher Oktoberfest or Old Dominion Oktoberfest.

Before You Begin: If you have sensitive skin, wear rubber gloves when you work with hot peppers.

3 lb boneless skinless chicken breasts
1 small Spanish onion, diced
1/2 tbsp chopped fresh or canned jalapeño peppers
1/2 cup diced green chili peppers
1/2 tsp hot pepper flakes
12-oz can each diced tomatoes and crushed tomatoes
1½ tsp each ground cumin and chili powder
1½ tsp each red wine vinegar and sugar
1 tsp dried oregano
1/2 tsp each salt and black pepper
1 large bag white corn tortilla chips
1 lb Monterey Jack cheese, grated
1/4 head iceberg lettuce, shredded
2 tomatoes, chopped
1 small onion, chopped
sour cream as needed

Grill or poach the chicken until it is firm and fully cooked. Set aside to cool.

In a large pan on medium heat, sauté the onion, chilies and hot pepper in oil until onion is translucent and peppers tender. Add tomatoes, cumin, chili powder, vinegar, sugar, oregano, salt and pepper, and mix well. When chicken is cool, cut into bite-size pieces and add to tomato mixture; simmer for 5 to 10 minutes.

To assemble the pie, cover the bottom of a casserole dish with chips and press down to flatten. Add some chicken mixture, cheese and more chips. Repeat the layering process until the pan is full. Bake in a 350°F oven for 20 minutes. Serve topped with lettuce, chopped tomatoes, onion and sour cream.

Serves 6.

Lamb Shanks Braised in Porter
with Fresh Thyme

From: Pyramid Alehouse & Thomas Kemper Brewery
Seattle, Washington, USA

Created by Chef Leslie Dillon

Shanks may be among the cheapest cuts of lamb, but the long braising time of this recipe brings out every iota of flavor for a delicious dish.

Beermate: Even after such an extended cooking time, the lamb will still have a fairly strong flavor and so requires a sturdy companion beer. Try a strong, malty ale like Old Jack Strong Ale or Icicle Creek Winter Ale.

Before You Begin: Because you will use only a small amount of the braising liquid when you serve the shanks, what remains will make the base of a terrific soup. Just add a cup of pearl barley or rice to the leftover broth, let simmer for an hour or so and—voila!—soup for tomorrow's lunch.

2 tbsp olive oil
4 lamb shanks
salt and pepper
1½ cups finely chopped onions
1 cup finely chopped carrots
1 cup finely chopped celery
1 cup seeded and finely chopped tomato
2 tsp minced garlic
3/4 cup porter
3 cups beef stock
2 bay leaves
1 tsp salt
1 tbsp minced fresh thyme

Heat the olive oil on medium in a shallow pan large enough to hold all four lamb shanks. Brown the shanks well in the oil and season to taste with salt and pepper. Add the onions, carrots and celery and sauté until onions are translucent. Add the tomato and garlic and stir well. Remove vegetables from the pan and set aside. Deglaze the pan with the porter and return the vegetables along with the beef stock, stirring well. Stir in the bay leaves, salt and thyme and bring to a boil.

Cover the pan and simmer for 2 to 2½ hours until the meat is tender. If necessary, replenish with water while cooking.

Serves 4.

Pike Pale Ale and Oregon Honey
Marinated Rack of Lamb

From: The Pike Pub and Brewery
Seattle, Washington, USA

Created by Chef Nathan Ojala

This recipe accounts for the second most ingenious way I know of to use barley malt — after brewing, of course.

Beermate: The sweetness of the honey leads me to recommend a Scotch ale such as McAndrew's Scotch Ale or Sailor Hägar's Wee Heavy.

Before You Begin: Light roast barley malt can be purchased from a local home-brewing shop. Ask your butcher to do a French cut on the rack of lamb, which means cutting individual ribs, leaving the top rib bone on and exposed.

10-rib rack of lamb, French cut
1/2 cup honey
3/4 cup light roast barley malt
3 cups pale ale
1/4 cup chopped fresh mint
1½ cups water
3/4 cup honey
1/3 cup vegetable oil

Cut the rack of lamb into individual ribs and coat one side of each with honey, and then with the barley malt.

In a large bowl, combine the pale ale, mint, water and honey. After the lamb has been encrusted with the barley, wrap each rib bone individually in foil and place in a roasting pan. Pour the marinade over the ribs and let sit refrigerated for at least 6 hours.

Place the oil in a heavy-bottomed pan on medium-high heat. When the oil is very hot, sear each side of each rib and transfer the seared ribs to a broiler pan. Roast the lamb in a 400°F oven until done, basting with the leftover marinade every 5 minutes or so.

Serves 10.

Seared Rabbit Legs with Mustard-Mushroom-Thyme Sauce

From: Dock Street Brewing Company
Philadelphia, Pennsylvania, USA

Created by Chefs Richard Barlow and Paul Trowbridge

If you have never enjoyed the succulent flavor of rabbit, this dish is a perfect place to begin.

Beermate: The full flavors of this dish require a companion beer that is full-bodied but not overly sweet. A well-constructed porter seems just the thing, perhaps an Elora Grand Porter or a Black Butte Porter.

Before You Begin: Rabbit is best served medium-rare and if it cooks too long, it will toughen. Keep a close eye on the legs to make sure that they do not over-cook. If it looks like that might happen, remove from the oven and wrap in foil until the sauce is finished.

12 rabbit legs
Flour seasoned with salt and pepper as needed
Olive oil
2 bunches fresh thyme, chopped
10 shallots, peeled and sliced into rings
1/4 cup minced garlic
2 Spanish onions, julienned
8 cups coarsely chopped wild mushrooms
8 cups white wine
2 cups whole grain mustard
Salt and pepper to taste

Place a large, heavy-bottomed pan on medium-high heat and cover the surface with oil. When the oil is hot, dredge each rabbit leg in the seasoned flour and sear in the pan until browned, then flip and brown the other side.

Place the legs in a baking dish in a 375°F oven and cook until done. Meanwhile, reduce the heat in the pan to medium and add 1/4 cup olive oil, the thyme, shallots and garlic. Sauté for about 3 minutes before adding the onion. Sauté until onion is translucent; add mushrooms and sauté for 10 minutes.

Deglaze the pan with the wine and reduce by one quarter. Add the mustard and season with salt and pepper. Serve the rabbit legs topped with sauce.

Serves 12.

Denver Venison in a Mandarin Pineapple Salsa

From: Marin Brewing Company
Larkspur, California, USA

Created by Chef Matt Fluke

While venison is certainly more common today than it was even five years ago, it is still enough of a rarity to surprise and please most guests at a summer barbecue. And if the venison alone doesn't impress them, this wonderfully fruity salsa certainly will.

Beermate: For plain grilled venison, I would normally recommend a light ale such as an amber or mild brown ale. With the sweetness and acidity of the salsa, however, I think that one of the hoppier American versions of a brown ale would be more appropriate, perhaps an Oregon Trail Brown Ale or Pete's Wicked Ale.

Before You Begin: "Denver cut" means that the bone has been removed, which in this case means leg meat without the bone. If you want to simplify matters, ask your butcher to cut the venison into 8 servings of roughly 8 oz each.

For the Salsa:
2 cups drained mandarin orange segments
2 cups drained and diced pineapple
1/2 cup chopped green onions
1/4 cup honey
1/2 cup unsweetened pineapple juice
1 tsp salt

4 lb venison, Denver cut

In a mixing bowl, combine the oranges, pineapple, onions, honey, pineapple juice and salt and mix well. Cover and place in the refrigerator for at least 1 hour so that the flavors can blend.

Cut the meat into 8-oz portions. In a sauté pan on medium-high, heat a small amount of vegetable oil and brown each piece of meat on all sides. Transfer the meat to a hot grill and cook until medium-rare. (Instead of grilling the meat, it can be cooked in a 375°F oven for 5 to 10 minutes.)

Serve each piece of venison with about 1/2 cup of salsa.

Serves 8.

MARIN BREWING COMPANY
1809 Larkspur Landing Circle
Larkspur, California, USA 94939
Phone: 415-461-4677

If, like me, you are one of those odd beer aficionados who are particularly fond of well-made fruit beers, there are three places you must visit: Frank Boon's lambic brewery in Lembeek, Belgium, the Liefmans Brewery in Oudenaarde, Belgium, and the Marin Brewing Company in Larkspur, California. At Boon, you will taste some of the finest cherry- and raspberry-flavored lambics that Belgium has to offer. At Liefmans, you will learn that the Belgians are highly skilled at adding fruit to Flemish brown ales as well as lambics. And at Marin, you will get a taste of where all of these New World fruit ales began and discover why some of them are so good.

Just across the Golden Gate Bridge from San Francisco lies Marin County, and within it is situated the tiny town of Larkspur, home to Marin Brewing. When I first visited the brewpub with Tom Dalldorf, the publisher of the *Celebrator Beer News*, I was struck by how inconspicuous the place looked as we approached it in Tom's van. True, it appeared quite pleasant, set out as it was against the backdrop of the Larkspur Landing ferry terminal with San Quentin Prison lurking ominously overtop, but there was certainly no indication of the kind of eccentricity one might expect from a place known for its fruit beers. Even as we entered the pub, it all looked so, well, normal.

There was nothing normal, however, about entering a blueberry-flavored ale at the Great American Beer Festival in 1990, only the second year that the competition had a fruit beer category. And there was certainly nothing normal about winning the gold medal that year, the year after that and then again two years later. But this is exactly what Marin Brewing did, and in so doing, the brewpub and their then-brewer, Grant Johnson, helped to define and popularize the North American fruit beer style.

Personally, I will normally associate that kind of pioneer spirit with at least a certain degree of off-the-wall attitude, but Marin demonstrated no more of that characteristic than any other brewpub I had visited. This I found somewhat curious, or at least, I did until I tasted Johnson's other beers. Sips of a splendid Mt. Tam Pale Ale and a lovely, mocha-ish Breakout Stout were more than enough to convince me that while the fruits may have given Marin some degree of infamy, this brewpub has a lot to offer to even the unwavering British beer partisan. Indeed, there is nary a stiff upper lip that would not quiver at a taste from a fresh glass of Point Reyes Porter.

So, yes, Marin remains on the list of must-sees for fruit beer lovers. But once you have enjoyed your Bluebeery Ale, Stinson Beach Peach and Raspberry Trail Ale, settle down for a pint of pale, as well, and learn that eccentricities can also be quite dignified.

BREADS

Beer Bread

From: Swans Hotel and Pub/Buckerfield's Brewery
Victoria, British Columbia, Canada

Created by Chef John Gallichan

A lovely bread for sandwiches, French toast made with eggs and maple-flavored beer or eating plain or with butter at lunch or dinner.

Beermate: It is said that good bread goes with good beer, and in this case, it might be added that almost any good beer will accompany this bread expertly. For a basic cheddar cheese sandwich, though, I will go out on a limb and suggest a moderately hoppy brown ale such as Red Nectar or Samuel Adams Boston Ale.

Before You Begin: The lack of rising time (if you use the quick yeast) means that this bread can be made fresh and hot in about an hour's time, which makes it as convenient a bread recipe as you can find.

5 tbsp white sugar
5 tbsp vegetable shortening
2 pinches salt
2 tbsp quick yeast (or 4 pkgs dry yeast)
4 cups pilsner or light ale, at room temperature
12 cups all-purpose flour

In a large bowl or a food processor with a dough mixer, combine the sugar, vegetable shortening, salt and yeast. Add the warm beer and mix well.

Add the flour a bit at a time, making sure that it is fully mixed in before adding more. Turn the dough out of the bowl about halfway through (if not using a processor) and continue adding the flour and working it into the dough until the dough is no longer sticky. If using a food processor, continue adding the flour with dough mixer running until the proper consistency is achieved.

(If you are using dry yeast instead of quick yeast, return the dough to the bowl, cover with a clean tea towel and place in a warm spot for about 1 hour. Beat down the dough, form it into loaves, cover and let rise for another hour or two, until doubled in size, before baking.)

Separate the dough into 4 parts and form each part into a round and place on a baking sheet. Slash the top with a sharp knife and bake in a 350°F oven for 40 to 45 minutes or until done.

Makes 4 loaves.

Edgefield Beer Bread

From: McMenamins Edgefield Estate / The Black Rabbit Restaurant
Troutdale, Oregon, USA

Created by Chef Geri Marz

A sort of muesli bread without fruit and nuts, this is both filling and fulfilling—make lots!

Beermate: A rich bread such as this will generally call for a similarly rich beer, say an Anchor Porter, the Catamount Porter or whatever beer you used in the recipe. For a fun variation, though, serve it with the beer that was made from the spent grain.

Before You Begin: Take a container in hand and wander down to your local brewpub to ask for a cup of spent grain (malted barley that has been used in brewing). If you get there before the farmer who inevitably picks up the grain to use as feed, the brewer will probably be happy to give you some. Failing that, use 1/2 cup of bran in its place.

> 2½ cups stout or porter, at room temperature
> 2 tbsp brown sugar
> 2 tbsp dark molasses
> 1½ tsp dry yeast
> 1 cup cracked wheat
> 3 cups all-purpose flour
> 2 cups whole wheat flour
> 1 cup spent grain
> 2/3 cup sunflower seeds
> 1 tbsp salt
> 1 egg
> 2 tbsp water

Combine the stout, sugar, molasses, yeast and cracked wheat in a large bowl and let stand for 10 minutes. Add both types of flour, the spent grain (or bran), sunflower seeds and salt and knead the dough for ten minutes. Form the dough into 2 loaves and place in greased 9 x 5-inch loaf pans, slashing the tops end to end with a sharp knife. Beat the egg along with the water and brush this wash over the tops of the loaves. Cover with a clean tea towel and let stand in a warm place until doubled in size. Bake in a 425°F oven for 15 minutes. Reduce heat to 350°F and continue baking for a further 25 to 30 minutes or until a knife inserted in the middle comes out clean.

Makes 2 loaves.

Jalapeño Beer Bread

From: Pepperwood Bistro
Burlington, Ontario, Canada

Created by Chef Tina Dine

Whatever it is that links hot peppers to beer, in the immortal words of Martha Stewart, it's a good thing. This easy-to-make, no-rise bread is a simple and tasty addition to any party platter, but I like to keep it for myself.

Beermate: The frying of the jalapeño takes away much of its heat, so its role in this bread is more for flavor than spice. As such, a lightly hoppy cream ale like Sleeman Cream Ale or a hoppy Vienna lager such as the Brooklyn Lager will make a fine partner.

Before You Begin: It's a good idea to sauté the jalapeño first and let it cool on a paper towel while you are assembling the other ingredients.

3 cups all-purpose flour
5 tsp baking powder
3 tbsp white sugar
1½ tsp salt
1½ cups abbey-style Belgian ale
½ cup shredded medium cheddar or Monterey Jack cheese
1 small jalapeño, minced and sautéed

Place the flour, baking powder, sugar and salt in a large bowl and mix well. Add the beer, cheese and pepper and blend together thoroughly. Pour the batter into a greased 9 x 5-inch loaf pan and bake in a 350°F oven for 1 hour. Butter the top of the loaf while it is warm and serve.
Makes 1 loaf.

Beer and Oat Bread

From: The Kingston Brewing Company
Kingston, Ontario, Canada

Created by Chef Roger Holmes

The pale ale does add a little bitterness to this bread, which I personally enjoy, but if you do not want that quality in your bread, use a sweeter ale such as brown ale or mild.

Beermate: This unique bread is great on its own accompanied by a glass of good oatmeal stout, such as the Barney Flats Oatmeal Stout. Or add smoked ham and hot mustard for a tasty sandwich to be relished with a dry stout like Guinness.

Before You Begin: Bread takes time, so don't rush it. When you are adding the flour to the dough, do it slowly and a better loaf will result.

4 cups rolled oats
5 cups all-purpose flour
2 tbsp dry yeast
1½ cups warm water (100°F)
1½ cups pale ale (moderate hoppiness)
1/2 cup dry milk powder
1/2 cup brown sugar
1 tbsp salt
1 tbsp oil

First, process 2 cups of rolled oats in a blender or food processor until it looks like coarse flour and toast the remaining 2 cups on a cookie sheet in a 350°F oven until golden. (The toasting will take approximately 20 to 30 minutes.) While the oats are toasting, combine in a bowl 1 cup of flour, the yeast and the warm water. Cover and allow to rest in a warm place for 15 minutes.

In a second larger bowl, combine the pale ale, dry milk powder, brown sugar and salt. Pour in the yeast mixture and mix well with a spatula. Stir in 3 cups of flour and the toasted and ground oats, reserving the last cup of flour. When well mixed, add just enough of the last cup of flour to prevent the dough from sticking to the sides of the bowl. Knead the dough until it is smooth and elastic. Coat another bowl with oil and turn dough over in this until it is covered with the oil. Cover and allow to rise in a warm place until doubled in size. (This will take about 15 to 30 minutes, depending upon the yeast used.)

Cut the dough in half and shape into loaves. Throw loaves firmly onto the counter to get out any air bubbles and place in greased 9 x 5-inch loaf pans to let sit until doubled again. (This will take slightly longer than the first doubling, about 30 to 40 minutes.)

Bake in a 350°F oven for 20 to 30 minutes, or until a knife inserted in the middle comes out clean.

Makes 2 loaves.

THE KINGSTON BREWING COMPANY
34 Clarence Street
Kingston, Ontario, Canada K7L 1W9
Phone: 613-542-4978

Rightly or wrongly, Canadians living in the eastern half of the nation tend to look at the provinces of Ontario and Quebec as composing the heart of the country. It is an understandable conclusion. Nearly two-thirds of the total population of Canada resides in the area known as Central Canada and the major cities of these two provinces, Montreal, Quebec, and Toronto, Ontario, are by far the largest in the land. As such, the first brewpub that opened in either province must by definition be a significant and historic entity. That brewpub was The Kingston Brewing Company.

In truth, it is somewhat inaccurate to call the KBC the first brewpub in Ontario. The fact of the matter is that brewpub licence number one actually went to an establishment known as the Atlas Brewpub and Entertainment Complex, located in Welland near Niagara Falls. Due to the somewhat unsavory reputation of the Atlas, however, the Ontario government was reluctant to use it as their premiere brewpub for publicity purposes and instead turned all of the attention on The Kingston Brewing Company, which opened hot on the heels of the Atlas. Or at least, so the story goes.

Today, the Atlas is long gone as a brewpub and everyone in the province who cares about such things recognizes the KBC as the first brewpub of the modern era in either Ontario or Quebec. While that judgment of history may not be altogether fair, it certainly is appropriate, as the city of Kingston is itself steeped in history and the KBC is about as comfortable and neighborly a brewpub as anyone could ask for. In retrospect, it is almost as if the government had prearranged a custom-tailored, showpiece brewpub to be the province's first.

As Kingston is but a three-hour drive from my home in Toronto, I have visited the KBC on numerous occasions. On the drive to Montreal, the brewpub serves as an ideal midway lunch spot, and for weekend getaways, there are few cities as attractive and alluring as Kingston. The visit I remember best, however, was neither rest stop nor pleasant summer's respite; it was a weekend visit in February, during some of the most vicious winter weather that was visited upon Ontario all that winter.

The occasion was the opening of an art show in which my wife, Christine, was participating. We had made all of the arrangements well in advance, including a room in a delightful historic hotel, and when the bad weather hit, we boldly, and I suppose obliviously, forged ahead. Fortunately, we made it to Kingston in one piece.

Although the weather limited the art opening to a rather sparse attendance, the hearty people of Kingston still managed to keep the KBC hopping all weekend long. I know this because with our hotel located just across the street, the brewpub proved to be our near-exclusive choice for dining and entertainment. I was not surprised, though, for good brewpubs have a habit of drawing people to them, no matter what the weather.

Jalapeño and Cheddar Cornbread

From: C'est What Brewery, Winery and Restaurant
Toronto, Ontario, Canada

Created by Chef Jeff Sararas

A remarkably colorful, spicy and flavorful cornbread, this is just the thing to provide a warm southern feel on cold, northern, midwinter days.

Beermate: The cheese and the vegetable oil make this bread a little on the oily side, so try juxtaposing the hoppiness of an American pale ale like the Red Seal Ale or the Pyramid Pale Ale.

Before You Begin: This bread, like all cornbread, is at its best when served warm, straight out of the oven if possible. If you do not eat it all at once, you can store it for up to a day or two in the fridge and reheat before serving. In place of the buttermilk, the same amount of half-and-half or milk may be substituted, but it should first be curdled by stirring in 1 tbsp of lemon juice or vinegar. And if you find that the butter pools on the top of the baking bread, wait until the bread has formed a crust then tilt the pan just enough to let the butter run off to the sides.

1 cup grated cheddar cheese
1 cup each kernel corn and cornmeal
3/4 cup finely diced red and green peppers
1 tbsp minced jalapeños
3/4 tsp baking soda
1/2 tsp salt
1/2 cup buttermilk
1/2 cup vegetable oil
1 large egg
2 tbsp butter

In a large bowl, combine half of the cheese, the corn, cornmeal, red and green peppers, jalapeños, baking soda, salt, buttermilk, oil and egg and mix well. In a 9 x 5-inch loaf pan or medium-size cast iron pan, melt the butter in a 350°F oven. When the butter is hot but not browned, remove from the oven and swirl it to coat bottom and sides. Allow the butter to pool in the bottom of the pan and scrape the batter into center of it. Sprinkle with the reserved cheddar and return to the center rack of the oven. Bake for approximately 35 minutes or until golden and a knife inserted in the center comes out clean. Place on a rack to cool. When ready to serve, loosen the sides and bottom with a thin knife or pie lifter and invert the bread onto a plate.

Makes 1 loaf.

Red Tail Pizza Crust

From: Mendocino Brewing Company
Hopland, California, USA

Created by Chef Jan Franks

A quick and easy pizza dough that doubles as a herb flatbread; just add a little extra virgin olive oil, a sprinkle of kosher salt and, of course, herbs to the top of the plain finished crust.

Beermate: This all depends, of course, on what you do with your crust. I always recommend Vienna lager for basic tomato-sauce pizzas, or a Bohemian-style pilsner if you are enjoying this dough as a flatbread.

Before You Begin: Remember that this dough does need a little rising time and plan your dinner accordingly. Perhaps the simplest thing to do is to make it well in advance and store in the refrigerator until needed.

1 pkg quick-rise yeast
1 tsp sugar
1 cup warm water
1 pkg quick-rise yeast
1 tsp sugar
3 cups all-purpose flour
1 cup brown ale
Extra flour as needed

In a small bowl, dissolve the sugar and yeast in the warm water and wait for the yeast to activate. When the yeast mixture begins to bubble, put the flour in a separate large bowl and mix in the beer and the yeast mixture. Add more flour if necessary to make a soft dough. Knead the dough for 5 minutes and then cover and let sit in a warm place for 30 minutes. Roll out the dough to form a crust and top with your chosen pizza toppings, or bake as a flatbread. Bake for 15 minutes in 400°F oven, or until golden brown.

Makes 1 pizza crust.

MENDOCINO BREWING COMPANY
13351 Highway 101 South
P.O. Box 400
Hopland, California, USA 95449
Phone: 707-744-1361

Many years ago, while on one of my infrequent trips to northern California, I was handed a bottle of ale by a kind soul about whom I unfortunately remember nothing. I do recall vividly the reaction I had upon tasting the beer, however, which was something along the lines of "What is this beer and why have I never tasted it before?" The beer was Red Tail Ale.

I have been a fan of Red Tail and its brewer, the Mendocino Brewing Company, ever since that revelation. At the time, of course, I had no idea that I was imbibing an American beer classic, but I know it now and have a profound respect for the great job that Mendocino does on not only the Red Tail, but also the Eye of the Hawk Special Ale, Blue Heron Pale Ale and Black Hawk Stout. They are a quartet of beers that make Mendocino worthy of legendary status.

But then again, the brewery would have been renowned even if the brewers at Mendocino were not to produce another drop from this day forward. This is because Mendocino, or more precisely, their Hopland Brewpub, was the first modern brewpub established in California and the second in the United States, beating the better-known Buffalo Bill's to the punch by a matter of weeks. And as if that were not legendary enough, there is still more.

The other piece of the legend puzzle concerns a brewing company called New Albion. Established in 1976, New Albion is generally credited with having been the pioneer of the craft-beer renaissance as the first modern microbrewery to open in North America. Unfortunately, it was also one of the first to close. When the doors shut for good in 1982, the spirit of New Albion lived on in Mendocino Brewing, which bought much of the pioneer micro's equipment while it was setting up and New Albion was shutting down.

While virtually all of that equipment has been mothballed in the intervening years, the allure of history lives on at the brewery. Although the ties that once bound these two companies in a much more tangible way now exist in a purely spiritual sense, they are ties nonetheless.

As for my ties to the brewery, I still don't know why it took me so long to sample the Red Tail or the precise details of how it was that I finally did get a chance to taste it. One thing I do know though, is that I owe a debt of thanks to that mysterious soul who handed me that fateful bottle.

DESSERTS

Apple Crisp

From: The Vermont Pub & Brewery
Burlington, Vermont, USA

Created by Chef Tom Dubie

The addition of lemon juice gives this crisp a wonderful sweet-and-tart character.

Beermate: In trying to pick a beer to marry with this dessert, I was stumped about whether to match the sour or the sweet characteristics of the crisp. In the end, I decided to do both with the choice of a raspberry wheat beer like the Sangre de Frambuesa or a Belgian framboise such as the Timmermans Framboise.

Before You Begin: Peeling the apples is purely a matter of preference for this dish; suit your own tastes.

For the Crisp:
4 lb McIntosh apples, peeled, cored and sliced
3 tbsp lemon juice
3 tbsp cinnamon
2 tbsp all-purpose flour
1/2 cup apple juice

For the Topping:
2 cups rolled oats
1½ cups all-purpose flour
1 cup brown sugar
4 tsp cinnamon
1/2 lb butter
Extra sugar and cinnamon as needed

In a large bowl, mix together the apples, lemon juice, cinnamon and flour. Pour the apple juice into an 8 x 8-inch square pan and pile in the apples. (Don't worry too much about the height of the apple mixture, it will settle during baking.)

In a separate bowl, mix together the oats, flour, sugar and cinnamon; cut in butter until topping is crumbly. Spoon on top of the apples, covering all areas. Sprinkle with sugar and a dash of cinnamon.

Bake in a 350°F oven for approximately 1 hour or until the topping is well browned and firm to the touch and the apples are bubbling on the sides.

Serves 8.

Coriander Peach Cobbler

From: The Redhook Ale Brewery and Forecasters Public House
Woodinville, Washington, USA

Created by Chef Isles and Richard Wallace

Coriander adds a unique flavor and aroma to this delicious cobbler.

Beermate: With the coriander and fruity flavor of this dessert, there can be but one beer companion: Belgian-style wheat beer brewed with curaçao, orange peel and coriander. Try a Thomas Kemper Belgian White or the fruitier Blanche de Bruges.

Before You Begin: Use the freshest peaches and apricots available for the best effect.

For the Filling:
2½ lb fresh peaches, peeled and cut into large chunks
1 lb fresh apricots, peeled and quartered
1/2 cup sugar
3 tbsp all-purpose flour
1/2 tsp freshly ground coriander seeds
1 tsp grated fresh ginger

For the Topping:
1½ cups all-purpose flour
3 tbsp sugar
1 tbsp baking powder
1 tbsp freshly grated orange zest
1/4 tsp salt
1/4 tsp freshly ground coriander seeds
1/4 cup unsalted butter, chilled and cut into small pieces
1 cup heavy cream

Combine all of the ingredients for the filling in a 9 x 5-inch baking dish.

To make the topping, combine the flour, sugar, baking powder, orange zest, salt and coriander in a bowl. Using 2 knives or a pastry blender, cut the butter into the flour mixture until it resembles coarse meal.

Add the cream all at once and stir until moist clumps form. Spread the thick dough over the fruit by dropping evenly spaced spoonfuls of it and smoothing them together with a spatula. Don't worry if the entire cobbler does not get uniformly covered.

Bake in a 350°F oven for 30 minutes or until it is golden on top and the fruit is bubbling at the sides.

Serves 6.

Iced Lindemans Framboise Lambic Soufflé

From: The Pike Pub and Brewery
Seattle, Washington, USA

Created by Chef Nathan Ojala

A lovely, light dish that may be used as an intermezzo or dessert with equal success.

Beermate: This refreshing soufflé gets its flavor from the framboise lambic, so it only makes sense that it should be enjoyed with the same style of beer, such as a Lindemans Framboise or a Jacobins Framboise. For an interesting contrast, you could serve it with a different framboise from the one used in its preparation.

Before You Begin: To make the soufflé collars, simply wrap a piece of waxed paper around the outside of each cup and secure it with an elastic band. Just don't make the elastic too tight or it will snap in the freezer.

8 egg yolks
1¼ cups sugar
2 oz unflavored gelatin
1 cup warm water
2 cups framboise lambic
4 egg whites
1¾ cups heavy cream
six 5-oz soufflé cups

Beat the egg yolks with 1/2 cup of the sugar. Dissolve the gelatin in the water and add to the yolks and sugar. Transfer the mixture to the top of a double boiler and warm over simmering water until thick enough to coat the back of a spoon. Remove from the heat and stir in the framboise lambic.

Place the mixture in the refrigerator for 30 minutes or until it becomes syrupy. In a bowl, beat the egg whites until stiff peaks form. In a separate bowl, whip the cream. Fold the cream into the syrup first and follow it with the egg whites. Mix only until the lumps are dissolved—do not overmix.

Pour the mixture into soufflé cups so that it rises to 1 inch above the rims of the cups. Freeze for at least 1 hour.

Serves 6.

Sabayon with Riley's Scotch Ale

From: Swans Hotel and Pub/Buckerfield's Brewery
Victoria, British Columbia, Canada

Created by Chef Thanh Huynh

An exceptional and almost ethereal dessert that is given a lift with the clever addition of Grand Marnier and Scotch ale.

Beermate: Given the minimal ingredients in this dish, it doesn't take rocket science to deduce that Scotch ale might be its best accompaniment. Try the McRogue Scotch or the Traquair House Ale.

Before You Begin: The sabayon, or Italian zabaglione, should be made right before being served, so that it is warm and frothy when it comes to the table. If you wish to prepare it in advance, however, it may be frozen in custard cups and presented as frozen sabayon.

4 egg whites
5 tbsp sugar
1/4 cup Scotch ale
2 tbsp Grand Marnier

In a double boiler over low heat, whip together the egg whites and the sugar until stiff peaks begin to form. While still gently whipping, slowly add the Scotch ale and Grand Marnier. Continue to whip until the desired consistency is reached; serve immediately on its own or with fresh fruit.

Serves 4.

Albion Amber Tart

From: Marin Brewing Company
Larkspur, California, USA

Created by Chef Matt Fluke

This beery version of the French *tarte au sucre*, or sugar pie, is a sweet-tooth's dream.

Beermate: In my birth province of Quebec, a version of sugar pie is made with maple syrup and so my gastronomic memory has always linked the two flavors. This leads me to what I think is the perfect match for this tart, namely a strong, maple-flavored beer like the Niagara Falls Maple Wheat or the lighter Tommy-knocker Maple Nut Brown Ale.

Before You Begin: If you wish, Chef Fluke advises that a fruit-flavored beer may be used in place of the amber ale, but cautions that the the fruit taste will likely be lost in the baking of the dish.

2 cups all-purpose flour
1 tbsp sugar
Pinch salt
1/2 cup butter
Ice water
1¾ cups packed brown sugar
2 large eggs
1 cup amber ale

In a large mixing bowl, combine the flour, sugar and salt and mix well. Using 2 knives or a pastry blender, cut half of the butter into the mixture and add just enough ice water to bind the dough. Chill for 30 minutes.

Roll out the dough onto a floured surface until thin enough for a crust and line a tart tin with the pastry. Sprinkle the dough with the brown sugar.

In a bowl, mix together the eggs and beer until blended. Pass the mixture through a strainer directly over the pastry dough. Cut up the remaining butter and scatter over the tart.

Cook the tart in a 425°F oven for 35 minutes or until firm to the touch. Let stand for 10 minutes to set before serving.

Serves 6 to 8.

Ginger, Pear and Macadamia Nut Tart

From: Gordon Biersch Brewing Co., Inc.
Pasadena, California, USA

Created by Corporate Chef Kelly Degala

This recipe yields a deliciously aromatic tart that reminds me a bit of an Asian-influenced Tarte Tatin — served upright, of course.

Beermate: The complementary taste of a ginger-flavored beer such as the Golden Prairie Honey Ginger Beer would be wonderful with this dish, but if no such brew is available near you, try a strong golden ale such as Duvel or La Fin du Monde.

Before You Begin: This recipe makes enough for two 10-inch tart shells, so you can either double the filling recipe and make two tarts or freeze half of the dough for later use.

For the Tart Crust:
2½ cups all-purpose flour
3/4 cup sugar
1 cup unsalted butter
2 egg yolks
1/4 cup heavy cream

For the Filling:
4 pears
White wine as needed
1/2 cup unsalted butter
Peeled and chopped fresh ginger to taste
1/2 cup all-purpose flour
2 tsp ground ginger
2 eggs
3/4 cup sugar

In a large bowl, mix the flour and sugar together. Using 2 knives or a pastry blender, cut the butter into the flour until the mixture resembles coarse meal.

In a separate bowl, whisk together the egg yolks and cream. Add the flour mixture to this and mix until the dough is moist enough to be gathered into a ball.

Knead the dough twice only on a lightly floured surface, being careful not to use too much flour. Form the dough into 2 balls, wrap each in plastic and refrigerate for at least 2 hours. (If half is to be frozen, it should not be placed in the freezer until after it has been refrigerated.)

Begin making the filling by gently poaching the pears in a mixture of white wine and ginger. When softened but still firm, core and halve the pears.

In a small pan, sauté the fresh ginger with the butter until brown and foamy. Strain the butter into a small bowl and set aside. In a separate bowl, combine the flour and ground ginger and set aside.

In a clean bowl, whisk together the eggs and sugar until combined. Beat in flour and ground ginger until well mixed and then, pouring in a slow, steady stream, vigorously mix in the butter.

Roll out the dough and line a tart pan. Slice the pears thinly and completely cover the bottom of the pan. Pour in the filling. Bake in a 375°F oven for 1 hour or until firm and browned. Cool and serve garnished with mint and whipped cream as desired.

Serves 10 to 12.

Goose Island's Cascade Pumpkin Brûlée

From: Goose Island Brewing Company
Chicago, Illinois, USA

Created by Consulting Chef Keith Korn

About a week's worth of foresight is necessary to make this wonderful brûlée.

Beermate: I would suggest a classic old ale of England, an aged Thomas Hardy's Ale or a seasonal strong ale like Geary's Hampshire Special Ale.

Before You Begin: You will have to go to your local homebrew supply store to pick up the Cascade hops — absolutely vital to the unique flavor and aroma of this dish.

1/2 lb Cascade hops
10 eggs
2 cups heavy cream
1 cup pumpkin or butternut squash, cooked and puréed
(canned pumpkin may be used)
1/2 cup each milk and sugar
2 vanilla beans, split lengthwise
Pinch each salt, nutmeg, cinnamon
1/2 cup brown sugar

Five days in advance, seal the unbroken eggs in an airtight container with the Cascade hops. Let sit in the refrigerator.

When the eggs are ready, place the cream, pumpkin, milk, sugar, vanilla, salt, nutmeg and cinnamon in a heavy-bottomed medium saucepan and bring to a boil over medium heat. Remove from heat and let sit for at least 1 hour.

Strain the mixture through a sieve, discarding the vanilla beans and gently pushing the pumpkin through. Pour 1/2 inch of hot water into a large baking dish, and place in a 300°F oven for 15 minutes. Separate the hop-scented eggs, reserving the whites for another use. Whisk the yolks into the cooked mixture and strain again through a sieve.

Pour the mixture into 8 brûlée dishes or soufflé cups. Place the cups in the hot water in the baking dish in the oven and bake until the custard sets, about 45 minutes to 1 hour. (The custard will be set when a knife inserted into the center comes out dry.) Remove the cups from the water bath and let cool at room temperature for 15 minutes. Cover and refrigerate for at least 1 hour or overnight.

To serve, sprinkle brown sugar evenly across the tops. Place the cups under a hot broiler for about 30 seconds or until the sugar is evenly caramelized. Serve immediately.

Makes 8 servings.

Cappuccino Pie

From: Globe Brewery & Barbecue Company
Globe, Arizona, USA

Created by Chef Candy Schermerhorn

When Candy gave me this recipe, she told me that it tastes the way great coffee smells. And she was absolutely right!

Beermate: Given a dessert this creamy and light, you want to be careful not to match it with anything too heavy or imposing, or else the beer will weigh down the pie. For that reason, I think that a chocolaty dry stout would be a lovely accompaniment to this dish, perhaps a Murphy's Irish Stout or the sweeter Beamish Genuine Stout.

Before You Begin: The "cold-brewing" of the coffee cream was Candy's own invention and it is a brilliant idea. Let the cream sit overnight if possible to bring out all of the rich coffee flavors.

For the Coffee Cream:
3½ cups whipping cream
1/2 cup fresh whole bean Mocha Java coffee

For the Cappuccino Filling:
4 oz extra-bitter chocolate, coarsely chopped
1/2 cup butter
1½ cups icing sugar
3 extra large egg yolks
1/3 cup Frangelico liqueur
1/4 cup Crème de Cacao liqueur
1 baked 10-inch deep-dish pastry piecrust

For the Cappuccino Topping:
1/4 cup unsalted butter, melted and thoroughly cooled
1¼ cups icing sugar
3 tbsp Frangelico liqueur
2 tbsp Crème de Cacao liqueur

To make the Coffee Cream, grind the coffee beans to an almost powdery texture. Stir the ground coffee into the whipping cream and allow to set in the refrigerator at least 6 hours or preferably overnight.

To make the Cappuccino Filling, melt the chocolate slowly over medium-low heat, stirring frequently. Remove from the heat and allow to cool to room temperature.

In a mixing bowl, beat the butter and sugar until light and fluffy. Add the egg yolks and chocolate and beat thoroughly. Using a whip or electric mixer, add 2 cups of the chilled Coffee Cream and the liqueurs to the chocolate mixture, whipping until stiff. Spread the chocolate mixture into the baked pie shell and refrigerate while making the topping.

To make the Cappuccino Topping, whip together the butter, sugar and the liqueurs until very stiff. Spread over the pie OR use a pastry bag to pipe the topping decoratively over the top. Return the pie to the refrigerator to set and keep refrigerated until ready to serve.

Makes 1 10-inch pie.

Safe Sex

From: C'est What Brewery, Winery and Restaurant
Toronto, Ontario, Canada

Created by Chef Jeff Sararas

Truly a dessert for the 1990s, this has become a C'est What favorite.

Beermate: There is a lot of sweetness in the chocolate and orange liqueur flavor of this dish, so a sweet, fruity strong porter would seem to be just the thing to accompany it. Try the Okanagan Olde English Porter or the Okocim Porter.

Before You Begin: This recipe can also be doubled and poured over a graham cracker crust in a springform pan for a terrific no-bake cake.

> 4 oz semisweet chocolate, shaved
> 2 tbsp espresso or strong coffee
> 1 tbsp Triple Sec or Grand Marnier liqueur
> 1 cup whipping cream
> 1 tsp vanilla
> 2 egg whites
> 1/4 tsp lemon juice
> 1/4 cup sugar

In a double boiler on medium heat, combine the chocolate, coffee, liqueur and a tablespoon of the whipping cream, stirring constantly until the chocolate is half melted. Remove from heat and continue stirring until chocolate is completely melted. Set aside and let cool until it reaches about body temperature (this can be checked by dipping a finger in it).

In a large bowl, combine the whipping cream and vanilla and beat with an electric mixer at high speed until firm peaks form, stopping before the cream begins to dry out. Set aside in the refrigerator.

In a clean, dry bowl, beat the egg whites at medium speed until they begin to froth. Add the lemon juice, increase the beating speed to high and gradually add the sugar in a steady stream. Continue beating until the whites hold a stiff peak.

Working quickly, pour the cooled chocolate mixture over the whipped cream and gently fold together with a broad spatula, carefully scraping the bottom and sides of the bowl regularly. When well combined, add the egg whites and continue to fold until fully incorporated. Pour into 5 wine glasses and chill about 1 hour before serving. Garnish with mint leaves or fresh fruit as desired.

Serves 4 to 5.

Double Espresso Chocolate Mousse
with Chocolate Curls

From: The Norwich Inn
Norwich, Vermont, USA

Created by Chef Terrence Webb

This magnificent mousse is a positive powerhouse of chocolate and coffee flavors.

Beermate: Any dish with this kind of chocolate and coffee intensity deserves a big stout to sit at its side, an imperial stout, to be precise. Try the Courage Imperial Russian Stout or the Spinnakers Imperial Stout.

Before You Begin: When folding the three mixtures together, it is important to use a light hand and proceed slowly. Otherwise, you risk losing the volume of your mousse.

22 oz semisweet chocolate, chopped
4 oz bittersweet chocolate, chopped
1/2 cup espresso
8 egg whites
Pinch cream of tartar
1/3 cup sugar
1½ cups heavy cream
Chocolate curls

Melt the two chocolates with the espresso in a double boiler over low heat until smooth. Remove from the heat and let cool to room temperature.

In a clean bowl, whip the egg whites and cream of tartar until they form semi-firm peaks. Gradually whip in small amounts of sugar until the entire amount is incorporated.

In a separate bowl, whip the heavy cream until it forms stiff peaks.

Fold one-third of the egg whites into the chocolate until fully blended, then pour the chocolate into the remaining egg whites and again fold until uniform. Finally, fold this mixture into the whipped cream until uniform.

Place the mousse in a pastry bag with a star tip and pipe into a glass of your choice or, less decoratively, spoon into serving glasses. Using a sharp vegetable peeler, peel off long curls from a block of semisweet chocolate to garnish the top.

Serves 6 to 8.

Hale's Chocolate Celebration Porter Cheesecake

From: Hale's Ales Brewery and Pub
Seattle, Washington, USA

Created by Chef Doug Courter

Growing up in Montreal, Quebec, amidst all of the city's great delis, I have had occasion to try perhaps more than my fair share of cheesecakes. And I can say without reservation that this is one of the very best!

Beermate: The use of sour cream in this recipe serves to temper the sweetness of the cake, so an overly sweet beer is not required here. What is needed is a full and chocolaty body, so try a robust stout like the Brooklyn Black Chocolate Stout or a fine barley wine such as Old Crustacean.

Before You Begin: Make certain that you have lots of free oven time available before you start this recipe; including the cooling-down period, it takes close to five hours!

For the Crust:
10 oz of chocolate cookies ground to a find crumb (Oreo type)
2 tbsp melted butter

For the Filling:
1¾ cups sugar
1 cup sour cream
3 tbsp cornstarch
3 lb softened cream cheese
4 eggs
1 cup porter
7 oz semisweet chocolate, melted and kept warm

First, make the crust by tossing the cookie crumbs with butter and press the mixture into the bottom of a 10-inch springform pan. If possible, first line the base of the pan with waxed paper to facilitate the removal of the finished cake.

To make the filling, combine the sugar, sour cream and cornstarch in a food processor or large bowl, blend well and set aside. In a clean food processor or a bowl, combine one-quarter of the cream cheese with 1 egg and one-quarter of the porter and blend until smooth. Gently mix the cream cheese mixture into the sour cream mixture and repeat the process with the remaining 3 batches of the cream cheese. After the final batch is blended but before it is added to the main mixture, add the still-warm melted chocolate and gently blend it in. Then transfer the final batch to the main mixture, mixing with a large rubber spatula in a figure-8 pattern to incorporate as little air as possible into the batter while still blending well.

Pour the batter into the prepared pan and tamp it down to release any air. Then bake the cake in a water bath to help retain moisture, first lining the exterior of the pan with a large piece of foil so that no water can seep in. Set the cake in a larger baking pan, place both in a 275°F oven and fill the pan with hot water. Bake for 1 hour, replenish the water and bake for 75 minutes longer. After baking, turn the oven off and without opening the door, allow the cake to cool in the oven for 2½ hours before storing it overnight in the fridge. Remove the pan collar and cut the cake with a wet knife warmed in hot water.

Serves 12 to 16.

HALE'S ALES BREWERY & PUB
4301 Leary Way NW
Seattle, Washington, USA 98104
Phone: 206-782-0737

It was during a seemingly innocuous visit to Seattle, Washington that I had the good fortune to stumble upon one of the Pacific northwest's great and, to my observation, largely unsung brewing treasures, Hale's Ales. Not that Hale's is some tiny, off-the-beaten-track brewpub, mind you; it is actually a large brewing company with locations in both Seattle and Spokane, Washington. As a draught-only brewery, however, Hale's is little known outside its Pacific northwest selling area, even among the most veteran beer voyagers.

While I had heard of Hale's prior to my trip west, I had not heard enough about it to schedule a visit into my brewery-filled itinerary. Indeed, oddly enough, through two days in Seattle, no one had even mentioned the brewery, its pub or the fact that they had only recently opened a new brewing facility. And then I entered one of the city's many fine beer bars, specifically the Hilltop Ale House, and discovered Hale's Special Bitter.

The bitter was advertised on the beer card as being served "Dublin-style," a nomenclature that was new to me and that immediately caught my eye. As the bartender explained, "Dublin-style" meant that the ale was poured through a nitrogen-pushed dispensing system, much the same way as Guinness is traditionally served. So while the phrase was new, the method was old. But I bought a pint anyway.

From the very first sip I was glad that I had. The bitter was marvelously balanced, with a light and sweetish fruitiness and a woody-leafy hop pairing off perfectly in a smooth and profoundly drinkable pint. I had the first inkling that a change in schedule might very well be in order.

The next day, as I spoke with Charles Finkel, the head of Pike Brewing and Merchant de Vin, I happened to mention the fine pint I had enjoyed the night before. He replied that Mike Hale (the Hale behind Hale's Ales) did indeed produce some very nice beers and suggested that if I had not scheduled it, I should definitely make time to go over there during my visit. After a couple of other queries about the food at the brewery restaurant had been answered with enthusiastic endorsements, I found myself on the phone with Mike himself, booking a lunch meeting at the brewery.

My time spent at Hale's that day was short, about two hours, but it was also extremely satisfying. The beer was delicious, the food plentiful and of excellent quality and the porter cheesecake that rounded out both myself and the meal was simply heavenly. Although I barely had a chance to meet Mike Hale because my late arrival had caused unfortunate appointment conflicts, I did feel that I had been given a chance to get to know the man, through his brewery, its food and his fine ales.

Black Forest Torte

From: Stoudt's Black Angus Restaurant
Adamstown, Pennsylvania, USA

Created by Chef Carol Stoudt

This wonderful cake is perfect for serving at parties, as it looks extremely elaborate but is actually fairly simple to prepare.

Beermate: Any more fruit flavor might just make this cherry-heavy dessert too much, so I am reluctant to recommend an estery ale for accompaniment. Instead, paying homage to the Black Forest, I'll suggest a chocolaty doppelbock such as the famed Paulaner Salvator or the Dock Street Illuminator.

Before You Begin: Three ingredients are key to the taste of this cake: the cocoa, the kirsch and the cherries. Try to use good-quality ingredients, particularly where these three are concerned, and use fresh cherries if at all possible.

For the Cake:
2 cups all-purpose flour
2 cups sugar
3/4 cup unsweetened quality cocoa powder
2 tsp baking soda
1 tsp baking powder
1 tsp salt
1 cup vegetable oil
1 cup dry stout or coffee
1 cup 2% milk
2 eggs, beaten
1 tsp vanilla

For the White Frosting:
1 cup milk
3 tbsp all-purpose flour
1/2 cup vegetable shortening
1 cup sugar
2 cups soft butter
1 tbsp vanilla

For the Assembly:
Kirsch or cherry brandy as needed
2 cups black bing cherries, stoned (if canned, drain well)
1 cup whipping cream
Chocolate curls

In a large mixing bowl, combine the flour, sugar, cocoa, baking soda, baking powder and salt. Add the vegetable oil and beat until fully mixed. Add the stout or hot coffee, milk, eggs and vanilla. Beat the mixture with an electric beater for 2 minutes at medium speed. Pour the batter into 2 greased and floured 9-inch cake pans and bake at 325°F for 40 minutes. When finished, turn the cake layers out of the pans and let cool.

While the cake is baking, make the frosting by first whisking the flour into the milk in a small saucepan. Cook over medium heat until thick, stirring constantly. Let cool and refrigerate for 1 hour. Combine the shortening, sugar, butter and vanilla and mix them into the chilled milk and flour mixture. Beat for 10 minutes with an electric beater at medium speed.

To assemble the cake, first moisten both layers liberally with kirsch. Spread all of the frosting evenly on top of one layer. Place half of the cherries on top of frosting, gently pressing them down into the frosting and cake. Top with the second layer. Whip the cream until stiff peaks form and gently blend in more kirsch. Spread the whipped cream on top of the second layer, heaping it in swirls and mounds as you go. Cover the whipped cream with the remaining cherries and chocolate curls, which are cut from a block of semisweet chocolate using a vegetable peeler.

Serve immediately or store chilled in the refrigerator.

Serves 12 to 14.

STOUDT'S BLACK ANGUS RESTAURANT
Route 272
Adamstown, Pennsylvania, USA 19501
Phone: 717-484-4385

If you look very closely at a map of Pennsylvania, just southwest of Reading, you will find a tiny black dot denoting a place by the name of Adamstown. And if you drive to the middle of Adamstown, you will come to a small brewery called Stoudt's Brewing Company. While from the outside nothing visible will give you cause to consider it, you will have just arrived at the emotional, if not physical, heart of northeastern US brewing.

Established in 1987 by the dynamic Carol Stoudt, Stoudt's Brewing has become an East Coast craft-brewing icon for a number of reasons. To begin with, Carol has mandated quality since day one, so that even in the beginning, when Stoudt's could probably have gotten away with selling mediocre lagers, authentic German-style pilsners were a constant from the tiny brewery. If that were not enough, Stoudt's made another claim to originality by having been one of the few lager-producing microbreweries from those early days of craft brewing, a legacy that they maintain today through a wide array of flagship German-style beers. Furthermore, in recognition that brewing should be fun as well as business, every year in June, Stoudt's hosts the brewing community at what may be the most flat-out fun beer festival in the east, the Great Eastern Invitational Microbrewery Festival.

The end product of this dedication to quality, innovation and a great time is that Stoudt's is respected not only by beer drinkers, but also by its peers within the brewing industry. Ask any brewer from the eastern United States (and many from the west) about good beer, and the chances are that the name Stoudt will come up somewhere in the conversation.

My first visit to Stoudt's was not what one might call an auspicious occasion. To begin with, the car I rented for the trip to Pennsylvania Dutch country turned out to be about two classes smaller than I had wanted, and as I was to discover that day, had been engineered with about as much road-handling ability as a child's toy! Of course, this would not have been a factor had the sunny weather in which I set out remained through the day, instead of turning into a severe thunderstorm complete with torrential downpours. Suffice it to say that by the time I arrived at Stoudt's, over an hour late, I felt as if I had just been put through the ringer and hung out to dry.

My distressed state of mind eased soon enough though, as I was warmly received, despite my tardiness. I was first shown through the brewery and then Carol took me around her husband Ed's Black Angus Restaurant, which predated the brewery by 25 years, and the adjoining Bier Garten, which opened in 1978. My only regrets were that the Garten was not in full swing and that my schedule called for me to soon depart. But then again, if leaving was easy, Stoudt's just wouldn't be Stoudt's.

Terminator Chocolate Torte

From: McMenamins Edgefield Estate /The Black Rabbit Restaurant
Troutdale, Oregon, USA

Created by Chef Geri Marz

"Terminator" refers to the name of the Edgefield Stout used to make this dish, not the effects of the torte or any Arnold Schwarzenegger movies.

Beermate: With the fruit and nuts combining so well with the chocolate in this dessert, I am led to look for a medium- to full-bodied ale to serve as an accompaniment, and preferably one with a light fruity-nutty character. The object of my search is a good porter such as the Catamount Porter or the Anchor Porter.

Before You Begin: This torte is wonderful on its own or sprinkled with icing sugar, or glazed with chocolate ganache.

1/2 cup dried sour cherries
1/2 cup dry stout
1 lb semisweet chocolate
1 cup butter
1/2 cup all-purpose flour
3/4 cup hazelnuts, toasted and ground
6 eggs
2 egg yolks
1½ cups sugar

Place the cherries in a large bowl and cover with stout. Cover and let sit overnight in the refrigerator.

In a double boiler on medium heat, melt the chocolate and butter.

In a separate bowl, mix together the flour and hazelnuts.

In a large mixing bowl, whip together the eggs, yolks and sugar until tripled in volume. Gently fold the mixture into the melted chocolate and butter mixture. Add the cherries and beer and gently mix. Add the flour and hazelnuts and carefully mix until the color is uniformly chocolate.

Pour the batter into a greased and floured 10-inch springform pan and bake at 350°F for 30 minutes. (The cake will still be very soft when done.) Let cool and chill overnight before turning out of the pan.

Serves 14.

Triple Black Cake with White Chocolate Sauce

From: The Redhook Ale Brewery and Forecasters Public House
Woodinville, Washington, USA

Created by Chefs Isles and Richard Wallace

The Wallaces refer to this as a dessert for all seasons and it is easy to see why. The cake is not so heavy as to be intimidating at a summer barbecue but is still rich and chocolaty enough to satisfy any midwinter craving.

Beermate: As this cake demonstrates, coffee and chocolate go together as naturally as, well, coffee and chocolate and stout. Try a rich, chocolaty stout with this dessert, perhaps Brock Extra Stout or Boulder Stout.

Before You Begin: If Redhook's Double Black Stout or other coffee-flavored stout is not available in your area, substitute 3 tbsp dry stout and 1 tbsp strong coffee or espresso in the cake recipe and use dry stout for the sauce.

For the Cake:
1 lb dark chocolate, chopped
1/2 cup butter
5 egg yolks
5 egg whites
1 tbsp sugar
1/4 cup coffee-flavored stout
4 tsp flour

For the White Chocolate Sauce:
3 egg yolks
3 tbsp sugar
2/3 cup milk
1/3 cup heavy cream
2 oz white chocolate, finely chopped
1 tbsp coffee-flavored stout

In the top half of a double boiler, melt the chocolate and butter. Remove from the heat, transfer to a mixing bowl and let cool until just warm. Whisk in the egg yolks, 1 at a time, beating well after each addition. In a separate bowl, beat egg whites with the sugar until stiff peaks form. Gently fold half of the whites into the chocolate mixture. Pour in the stout and sprinkle the flour over top of the mixture and then continue folding in the egg whites. Be very careful not to over-mix as this will break down the whites.

Pour the cake batter into a buttered and floured 9-inch cake pan and bake in a 400°F oven for 15 minutes. Remove from the oven and let cool slightly before removing from the pan. Allow to cool completely before cutting the cake.

To make the sauce, whisk the egg yolks and sugar together in a bowl and set aside. In a heavy saucepan on low heat, warm the milk and cream until almost simmering. Take 1/2 cup of the warm milk and cream and whisk into yolks. Whisk the egg yolks into the milk mixture and, stirring constantly, cook until it begins to acheive a sauce-like thickness. Remove from the heat and stir in the white chocolate and stout. Refrigerate the sauce until ready to use.

For presentation, make a pool of chilled sauce on a plate and top with a slice of cake. If desired, garnish with fresh berries.

Serves 8 to 12.

THE REDHOOK ALE BREWERY AND FORECASTERS PUBLIC HOUSE
14300 NE 145th Street
Woodinville, Washington, USA 98072
Phone: 206-483-3232

By now, I would expect that most craft-beer aficionados have heard of Paul Shipman or his brewing company, the Redhook Ale Brewery. Whether by dint of Redhook's status as a pioneering microbrewery, the controversy and mythology that surrounded the brewery's "strategic alliance" with Anheuser-Busch or Paul Shipman's occasionally quite public feuding with rival Jim Koch of the Boston Beer Company, Redhook has become one of the most recognized and talked-about craft breweries in the United States.

Of course, if it were controversy and feuding alone that got Redhook its status, there would be many, many more brewers out there flinging mud at their competitors. No, Redhook's first and, ultimately, greatest claim to fame is its beer, and Paul Shipman would be the first to tell you that this is exactly the way it should always be.

At the time a marketing and sales analyst working in the wine trade, Paul founded Redhook in 1981 along with partner Gordon Bowker, the latter also a founder of the Starbucks Coffee chain. The first pint was drawn some 15 months later and the Redhook success story was underway, with a first year production of a mere 1,000 barrels of beer.

Sales grew at a breathtaking rate and by 1986, Paul and Gordon found themselves running short of production space. Never ones to rush into anything, the duo launched a search for a new space close to the original site and, more importantly for the sake of the beer, also began checking out new state-of-the-art brewing equipment. Eventually both were found and Redhook moved down the road from the Ballard district of Seattle to Fremont, where the brewery and the Trolleyman Pub still stand today.

The charms of the Trolleyman are considerable. Upon entering the front door, you are immediately greeted with the menu of the day, scrawled in marker upon an erasable board; over in the corner are comfortable chairs and a couch, as well as a working fireplace; the food is as homey as the beers are tasty; and the service is good-natured and efficient. It is indeed the kind of place where one could hunker down for the evening on a cold, rainy Seattle winter night.

Redhook's expansion continued after the Fremont move and the company has since set up breweries in Woodinville, Washington and Portsmouth, New Hampshire. The Woodinville site, located about 16 miles from the original brewery, houses the Forecasters Public House in addition to a large and thoroughly modern 200,000-barrel-capacity brewery.

Forecasters, where the Redhook recipes in this book come from, is in many ways the yang to the Trolleyman's yin. Much more elaborate than the Fremont pub, it is several times larger than the tiny Trolleyman and has obviously been much more carefully designed. Nonetheless, it still exudes a Trolleyman-like affability and the food, if anything, is even better than it is at the original pub. Most important, of course, the beers are just as authentically Redhook.

SAUCES &
CONDIMENTS

Hale's Celebration Porter Honey Mustard Dressing

From: Hale's Ales Brewery
Seattle, Washington, USA

Created by Chef Doug Courter

This sweetish, zingy dressing is a sure bet to perk up any salad. I particularly like it on a basic mixed salad of leaf lettuce, arugula and whatever interesting greens I can get my hands on.

Beermate: Sweet and flavorful with a light tang from the vinegar and a mild roastiness from the porter, this dressing on a green salad is lovely with a dunkel weizen at its side. Try an Erdinger Dunkel or a Schneider Weisse.

> 1¾ cups rough whole-seed country-style mustard
> 1 cup porter
> 2 tbsp white wine vinegar
> 6 tbsp olive oil
> 3/4 cup honey

In a medium-size bowl, combine all of the ingredients and mix well. Let sit, covered, in the refrigerator for 48 hours before serving. Store in a glass bottle or carafe.

Makes 4 cups.

Pub Apple Chutney

From: The Vermont Pub & Brewery
Burlington, Vermont, USA

Created by Chef Tom Dubie

A wonderful chutney from Vermont apple country, this is particularly fine on an autumn afternoon with fresh bread and strong cheese, or with sausages, chicken or pork, any time.

Beermate: Your choice of beer is largely dependent on what you serve this chutney with. For bread, cheese and chutney, try a best bitter like Fuller's London Pride. With pork or sausage, opt for a brown ale like Poppy Jasper Amber Ale.

Before You Begin: This recipe makes a lot of chutney, which is great if you love chutney but a bit of a problem if you have a small family and will only use it from time to time. Don't let that dissuade you, though, as jars of chutney make great gifts.

4 lb McIntosh apples, peeled, cored, thinly sliced and chopped
2 cups honey
2 cups vinegar
2/3 cup orange juice
3 tsp ground ginger
2 tbsp chopped fresh garlic
2 tsp cinnamon
2 tsp ground cloves
2 tsp salt
1/2 tsp cayenne pepper

Combine all ingredients in large saucepan and bring to a boil. Let the mixture simmer on low to medium heat for 1 hour and 45 minutes, stirring occasionally. Let cool before serving or refrigerating.

Makes approximately 6 cups.

Rogue Salsa

From: The Rogue Public House
Newport, Oregon, USA

Created by Chef Earl Smart

A simple, delicious and incredible colorful salsa that packs a punch!

Beermate: Forget all other flavors when matching a beer to this dish; the only thing that need concern you is the 3/4 cup of jalapeños. Pick a hoppy American pale ale to mellow the fire without killing the taste, perhaps a St. Ambroise Pale Ale or Humboldt Red Nectar Ale.

Before You Begin: If you can, try to use a chili beer that is ale-based, not a lager. If no such beer is available, you can make your own by stuffing a small, quartered jalapeño into a bottle of your favorite malty ale, recapping it and letting it sit in the refrigerator for a day or two before making the salsa.

2 lb tomatoes, diced, drained
1 large onion, diced
1½ cups chili beer (see above)
1 cup diced black olives
1 cup diced green peppers
1 cup diced yellow pepper
3/4 cup chopped jalapeños
1/2 cup chopped garlic
1 tbsp dried or chopped fresh oregano
1/2 tsp ground cumin
1/2 bunch coriander, chopped
Juice of 2 limes

In a large bowl, combine all of the ingredients and mix well. Let sit refrigerated for at least 2 hours in order to allow the flavors to blend. Warm to room temperature before serving.

Makes approximately 8 cups.

Hale's Ales Barbecue Sauce

From: Hale's Ales Brewery
Seattle, Washington, USA

Created by Chef Doug Courter

At the pub, they thin this sauce with a little water and simmer roast pork loin in it for a great-tasting sandwich. It is equally good as a marinade or barbecue sauce.

Beermate: Moderately spiced — by my standards, at least — and full of flavor, this sauce deserves a beer with a full body and moderate hopping. That means that on beef, I would call for a British pale ale; on pork, a moderately hoppy brown ale; and on chicken, a fine alt. Or in other words, something like Blue Heron Pale Ale, Full Sail Nut Brown Ale or St. Stan's Amber Alt.

Before You Begin: If you prefer, chili sauce may be substituted for the ketchup in this recipe, and feel free to add extra spice if you like your barbecue sauce hot.

6 tbsp butter
2 cups minced onions
2 tbsp minced garlic
1½ cups ketchup
2 cups tomato sauce
1/2 cup molasses
2 tsp salt
1½ tsp pepper
3 tbsp yellow mustard
1 tbsp lemon juice
2 tsp dried basil
1/2 tsp cayenne pepper
1 cup stout

In a heavy saucepan on medium heat, melt the butter and add the onions and garlic. Sauté until the onions are well wilted. Add the remaining ingredients to the pot and bring to a slow boil. Reduce to simmer and cook for about 45 minutes.

Remove the sauce from the heat and transfer to a blender or food processor to purée. Refrigerate overnight or until ready to use. (The sauce will keep in the refrigerator for about 10 days.)

Makes about 6 cups.

Old Peculiar Sauce

From: Granite Brewery
Toronto, Ontario, Canada

Created by Chef Clark Nickerson

All too often, we North Americans fail to pay enough attention to the gravies we make for our expensive cuts of beef. This rich, beer-flavored gravy offers a sure way to break that habit.

Beermate: Malty, flavorful Scottish ale is the perfect match for beef served with any gravy, and this particular sauce is no exception to that rule. Try the 5% alcohol by volume Maclay Scotch Ale or the less conventional but significantly stronger Loch Ness.

Before You Begin: If you want a creamier gravy, Chef Nickerson says that 1 tbsp of sour cream or a dollop of 10% table cream stirred in before serving will lend an even greater richness to the sauce.

1 onion, chopped
2 tbsp butter or margarine
1 tsp fresh rosemary (or 1/2 tsp dried)
1/4 cup all-purpose flour
1 cup water
1 tsp tomato paste
1 tbsp beef boullion
1 cup brown ale
1/2 cup fresh mushrooms, sliced
Salt and pepper to taste

In a saucepan on medium heat, sauté the onion in butter until translucent. Add the rosemary and flour and mix well to form a roux. Remove from the heat and set aside.

In a separate saucepan on medium, bring the water to a boil and reduce to medium-low heat. Dissolve the bouillon in the water and stir in the tomato paste. Bring back to a boil and add the ale. Simmer for 5 minutes, making sure not to boil.

Returning the roux to a low heat, slowly add the beer bouillon while beating with a whisk until smooth. If the sauce becomes too thick, add a little water until the desired consistency is reached.

Add the mushrooms and salt and pepper to the sauce and allow to simmer for approximately 20 minutes, stirring frequently.

Serves 4 to 6.

Roasted Garlic and Blue Cheese Ale Sauce

From: Spinnakers Brew Pub
Victoria, British Columbia, Canada

Created by Chefs George Chan and Stephen Engberf

This sauce is proof that a little good blue cheese will go a long way. Serve with grilled meat or on fresh pasta.

Beermate: Tossed with fresh pasta, this sweet, creamy sauce has a very pleasant tang from the cheese and an aromatic sweetness from the roasted garlic and sugar, so a sweetish and mildly roasty beer would seem to be just the right accompaniment. An Oktoberfest märzen such as the Hubsch Märzen or Full Sail Oktoberfest would be lovely.

Before You Begin: As long as you are roasting four cloves of garlic, you might as well do a full bulb so that you can have some for other dishes, too. To do this, simply chop the root off the bulb, drizzle the entire bulb with olive oil and follow the directions given below, using a baking dish in place of the foil if desired. Roasted garlic is also great spread directly on toast!

4 cloves garlic
1 tsp olive oil
Salt and pepper to taste
2 cups chicken stock
1 cup pale ale
1 cup whipping cream
1 small red onion, finely chopped
2 tbsp brown sugar (or 4 tbsp honey)
1 tbsp salt
Pinch black pepper
Pinch dried basil
1/2 cup crumbled blue cheese
Flour as necessary

Leaving their skins on, chop the root ends off the garlic cloves and toss them lightly with olive oil. Place the cloves on a piece of foil and dust lightly with salt and pepper. Close the foil to form a loose-fitting packet and bake at 325°F for about an hour. When the cloves are cool enough to handle, squeeze the roasted garlic paste out of the cut end and set aside.

In a saucepan on medium heat, combine the chicken stock, pale ale, whipping cream, onion, brown sugar, salt, pepper and basil and mix well. When the mixture is hot, add the cheese and stir until it is fully melted and incorporated into the sauce. Raise the heat to bring the sauce to a boil and then reduce the heat to simmer.

If necessary, whisk in a little flour at a time until the desired consistency has been reached. Simmer for 10 minutes before serving.

Makes approximately 4½ cups of sauce.

INDEX